MAINE LIVING

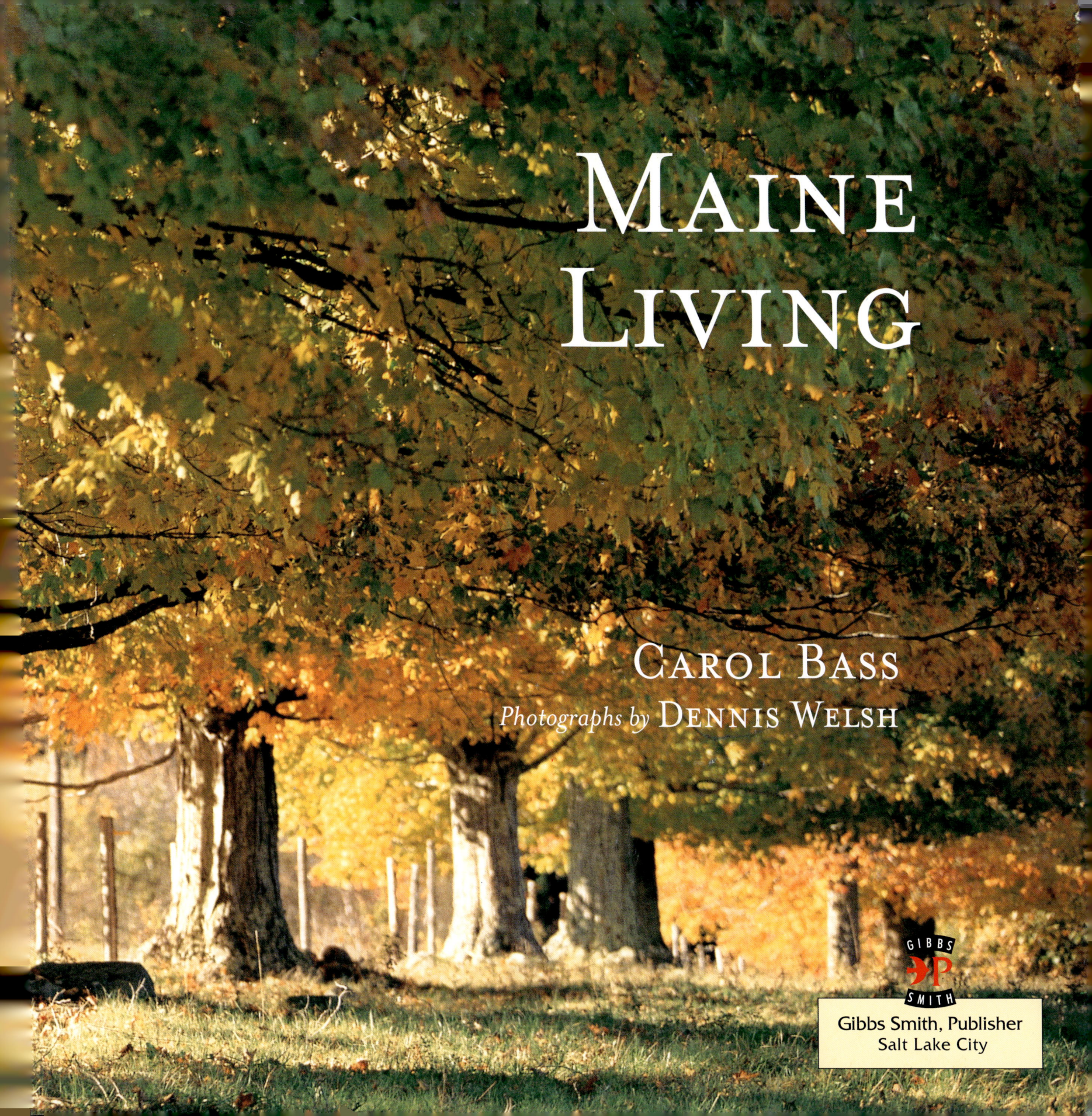

MAINE LIVING

CAROL BASS

Photographs by DENNIS WELSH

Gibbs Smith, Publisher
Salt Lake City

First Edition
08 07 06 05 04   5 4 3 2 1

Text © 2004 Carol Bass
All photographs © 2004 Dennis Welsh except: pages 57, 59, 62, 75, 76, 82, 83, 115, 166 © 2004 Carol Bass

All rights reserved. No part of this book may be reproduced by any means whatsoever without written permission from the publisher, except brief portions quoted for purpose of review.

Published by
Gibbs Smith, Publisher
P.O. Box 667
Layton, Utah 84041

Orders: 1.800.748.5439
www.gibbs-smith.com

Designed by Scott Santoro, Worksight, New York City
Printed and bound in Hong Kong

Library of Congress Cataloging-in-Publication Data

Bass, Carol
   Maine living / Carol Bass ; photographs by Dennis Welsh.—1st ed.
     p. cm.
  ISBN 1-58685-370-8
  1. Interior decoration—Maine. 2. Decoration and ornament, Rustic—Maine.
I. Welsh, Dennis. II. Title.
NK2002.B35 2004
747'.09741—dc22
                        2004008166

Dedication

*To the farmer in Cornville
and the townhall clerks,
the ferryboat captains,
the organic farmers,
the lilac growers,
the historical societies;
to the beekeepers,
the poets,
the musicians,
the storytellers,
the Maine Guides,
the apple-tree pruners . . .*

CONTENTS

Foreword   8

Introduction   10

Saltwater Nearby   16

An Ocean Inn   29

An Island Summer   37

Simple Structures   52

Passionate Work, Passionate People   63

Rural Landscapes   86

Inland Lakes   148

City Dwelling   159

Summer Festivals   167

Resources   174

Foreword

By Edgar Allen Beem

Carol Bass is well-known in Maine and beyond, as both a painter with a passion for bold colors and striking forms, and the creative force behind Maine Cottage Furniture, a design firm dedicated to bringing the casual elegance of the summer rich to the masses. Her own home on Littlejohn Island in Yarmouth, Maine, is as personal and idiosyncratic as the artist herself—an artful clutter of a cottage where it's sometimes difficult to tell where the artist's studio leaves off and her home begins. She is a woman possessed of natural style and an eye for overlooked beauty.

Most architecture and design books are armchair fantasies, impossible dreams calculated to allow readers and browsers to escape into the unobtainable preciousness of everything from Tuscan villas and English country homes to Japanese teahouses and Shaker meetinghouses. But Carol Bass is a realist. In *Maine Living*, she takes us on a journey in search of authenticity, an increasingly rare phenomenon in a consumer culture dedicated to and dominated by the virtual realities of television, motion pictures, and the Internet, and purveyors of the suburban sprawl such as big-box retailers that threaten to turn every place in America into "Anywhere, U.S.A."

Carol came to Maine from South Carolina in 1972. What she found here was one of America's last bastions of authenticity: a sparsely populated, heavily forested coastal state where nature and culture still maintained an uneasy balance, where most people still lived in small towns, and where even the "big" cities didn't have six-figure populations. The harsh Maine environment—long, dark, cold winters, thin soils, muddy springs—and Maine's relative remoteness from the centers of power and commerce have conspired over the decades to produce citizens who are hardy, self-reliant, independent, and tolerant. Mainers value their sense of community, but also prize their individuality. Out of this hard-bitten individuality comes a Maine style that is at once pragmatic and eccentric.

In *Maine Living*, Carol Bass looks beyond the high-style architecture and design of commuters and summer folks to discover the vernacular beauty of unpremeditated Maine in everything from clotheslines, tractors, and lobster boats to sheds, barns, cabins, porches, inns, and artists' studios. Everywhere she goes in Maine she draws out the stories attached to the places people have made their own, weaving them into an aesthetic of freedom. For Maine living is essentially about what it means to be free.

(Edgar Allen Beem is the author of *Maine Art Now* and *Maine: The Spirit of America* and a frequent contributor to *Down East, Yankee, Boston Globe Magazine,* and *Photo District News*. His weekly opinion column, "The Universal Notebook," appears in *The Forecaster*. A Maine native, he lives in Yarmouth with his wife and three daughters.)

Introduction

It's March first and the sun is spring-warm as I head out for a morning walk around the island with our pups Anna and Woody. We could yet be blasted with the wildest storm of winter, but spring is unmistakably on the way. A change in bird songs alerts me to the glorious return of the cedar waxwings.

Hundreds of these nomadic birds are hanging out in the swampy scrub bushes around Dorothy's yard. I can't see any buds yet, but the waxwings know that berries have been plentiful here in the past, and last summer's fermented meats offer a delicacy for these travelers. Their sporadic visits en route to breeding grounds in Newfoundland, Labrador and the Gaspé Peninsula herald spring—a full two weeks early this year.

Walking around the southeasterly side of the island, I meet Lisa, our neighbor, and report the waxwings' surprise return. For the past twenty years Lisa has roamed the world writing for travel guides. As we talk, a group of Canadian geese, bobbing among melting ice floes, honk and swim furiously away from the gregarious labs. An electric, right-out-of-the-paint-can cerulean blue sky meets the deep turquoise sea, and Lisa remarks as she does quite often, "There is no where else on earth like Maine. It's a place where the postcards really don't lie."

Gibbs Smith and I talked of producing a Maine book that captured a taste of the places that show a way of life difficult to find elsewhere. Maine, a geographical outpost thrust into the wild North Atlantic, has offered romance, mystery, retreat, and renewal to hundreds of thousands of people over the years.

In producing this book, I can put into words feelings I've had for years about this state; that Maine is a vast physical embodiment of a yearning all of us feel from time to time. In Maine we connect to the most primitive parts of ourselves; the DNA memory that goes way back to our time in caves, safe from the wooly bears outside, around fires inside.

Maine offers space to lose yourself, and discover a kind of isolation that invites contemplation and conveys mystery. Maine reflects our own inherent loneliness, our wild nature, our rejoining the earth. There is space enough and nature enough left to grow organic potatoes, make wild blueberry syrup, go clamming, or lie on pink granite in the sun. There is time to knit your own winter socks and build a fire for the sauna.

Afternoon popovers and tea are still being served on the lawn at the Jordan Pond House, as they have been since the late 1800s. Abby Vinal of Bremen bakes homemade blueberry pies that she sells at the end of her driveway. The Burning Tree Restaurant in Hull's Cove rivals anything in New York or San Francisco. The Chesuncook Inn, up near Baxter State Park, is open all year through. Craig Warren from Falmouth makes beautiful, laminated archery bows. Bill Gribbin, my neighbor, stands out on his porch at all hours practicing his bagpipes.

The wilderness of Cobscook Bay and Patten Pond beckons. Thoughts of camping in these sacred places nourish me through cold, dark January. Simply pronouncing the word "Meddybemps," a lake up in northern Maine, makes me happy. To know and understand that Meddybemps was a meeting place for Native American people during the Middle Archaic Period, 5500 to 4000 BC, as discovered by the University of Maine at Farmington archeology department, fills me with wonder.

I have been to Tuscany and I have been to South America. But driving through Cornville, Maine, on a late-September afternoon and stopping to buy fresh corn rates pretty high among my life's richest pleasures. I pass the farmer just as he unloads the day's pick from his tractor to his small roadside stand. A radio on a makeshift shelf plays country music. A rusty tin money box sits among the fresh-picked corn. Slanted sunrays golden up the pastures and make for the kind of afternoon my mother called "Technicolor Time." I stuff a paper bag with fresh ears a color green that artists swoon over and ride home toward supper. I nibble Maine's tastiest cottage cheese and goat cheese ever, from Nezinscot Organic Farm up in Turner, or lie down in an apple orchard near Strong or Madrid, and know I have truly been to heaven on earth.

Maine's backcountry roads, its "eggs for sale" signs, and its unacculturated ways inspire poet Wes McNair, a visiting professor of creative writing at Colby College and head of the creative writing program at The University of Maine at Farmington. Wes, known to write "poems for the back pockets of Americans," captures what so many of us feel about small-town Maine—and the graceful vernacular I hope you discover in these pages.

       Carol

WHERE I LIVE

You will come to an antique town
whose houses move apart
as if you'd interrupted
a private discussion. This is the place
you must pass through to get there.
Imagining lives tucked in
like china plates, continue driving.
Beyond the landscaped streets,
beyond the last colonial gas station
and unsolved by zoning,
is a road. It will take you
to old farmhouses and trees
with car-tire swings.
The timothy grass will run beside you
all the way to where I live.

                                        Wesley McNair

Alex Todd rows out to his boat, the Misty Jade, *on an early autumn morning.*

SALTWATER NEARBY

Harbor Fish

This book begins where the first Europeans landed, and where, every morning, the first light of day shines in this country—the Maine Coast. Custom House Wharf in Portland is truly a symbol of this state's long and vigorous fishing heritage.

This early-May morning the salty ocean air over the docks smells like salt sprinkled over a moist spring garden. Light sparkles on the edges of the buildings and shines on the storefront of Harbor Fish, waking up the street with bright colors. The pavement on the narrow street is worn away in spots, revealing the original granite cobblestone roadway.

For more than a hundred years there has been a fish market where Harbor Fish now stands. The Alfiero family has owned and operated Harbor Fish since the early 1970s.

Lobster boats make daily deliveries to the docks behind the market. From this bustling, tucked-away site, sweet Maine lobsters are distributed to restaurants and fish markets all across the country.

SALTWATER NEARBY

Porthole Restaurant

T en years ago, Oliver Keithy came to Maine and opened the Comedy Connection, a laugh-in nightclub, on Custom House Wharf. Since that time he has come to love the wharf and its people and is passionate about preserving life on the docks.

Several years ago he bought the Porthole, a Portland institution for at least eighty years. The ferries that serviced the islands always docked outside the Porthole before their recent move to a newer location several

Left: Eric Pray enjoys a hearty breakfast before heading out to sea. Eric lobsters with his father, Peter, during the summers, on their boat the Lady Catherine, named for Eric's sister. Fishermen have always named their boats after the women in their lives—daughters, wives, girlfriends—as a way of socializing the sea and honoring relationships. A boat named after a true love is thought to bring victory and success at sea.

wharfs away. The Porthole was the great gathering place for Casco Bay fishermen and islanders. It's still the best place to hear the latest news of the harbor.

The same counter and chairs have been here since the Porthole opened. "This place is sacred, a cultural jewel," says Oliver. "Why modernize or change anything that would interfere with this energy and spirit?"

Steven Johnson, Long Island boat builder and fisherman, enjoys a casual breakfast.

SALTWATER NEARBY

Man and Boat

Wandering around Custom House Wharf off Portland's Commercial Street, passing closed bars and open breakfast joints, your eyes land on a weathered, all-wood, double-ended sailing yacht. This boat stands out from just about every other boat in the harbor. One glance at its lines and continuous deck reveals a solid, seaworthy craft that brings to mind the lines of an ancient Viking ship. The boat is tied up to a lobster boat, which in turn is tied to the docks. Visiting the boat's owner requires a bit of nimble climbing through a jungle gym of ropes and booms, with a final leap onto sturdy wooden decks.

SALTWATER NEARBY 23

Grebe was constructed in the shipbuilding lands of Brittany, France, in 1933. Colin Archer, her designer, was a Norwegian naval architect born in 1832. He was well-known for his loveable, sea-worthy, double-ended styles.

Jeff can be found playing his banjo at local establishments, and walking home to Grebe *in the late evening. The camaraderie of the people working and living near the wharf provides a backdrop as rich and varied as any traditional homeowner enjoys.*

The salty yacht's name, *Grebe*, comes from an aquatic bird that builds its floating nests on the water. It's a suitable name, for *Grebe* has provided a floating year-round "nest" for its banjo-playing owner, Jeff Aumuller, since 1973. Jeff sails *Grebe* south every other season to warm his bones, but always returns to Maine, his true home berth.

Jeff's rustic manner and simple needs are reflected in the character of his boat. He prefers the decks oil-free and unvarnished, but bathes them constantly with buckets of salt water. This low maintenance wetting process results in wood weathered to a rich silver patina—much the same tone as Jeff's hair.

For years Jeff operated a canvas shop on the wharf, making and repairing sails. Several years ago he turned the shop over to his daughter Hannah, who runs a business producing lovely, functional, sailcloth totes.

Jeff survives the winter with heat from a tiny Yodel stove. Buckets placed under the stovepipe on the upper decks catch the condensation.

SALTWATER NEARBY 25

SALTWATER NEARBY

Harraseeket Lunch and Lobster

J ohn Coffin, co-owner of Harraseeket Lobster, walks the dock at the end of an October day. Harraseeket Lunch and Lobster is famous for outdoor, on-the-docks, right-off-the-boat steamed lobster from May through Columbus Day. They also market and ship lobsters all over the country, all year through.

BRING MAINE HOME

- Trade your dainty china for sturdy, "salt of the earth," colorful stoneware.

- Create a one-of-a-kind table: cover a flea-market tabletop with retro linoleum.

- Find metal-legged Deco diner stools, cover the seats with a bold-colored leather, and use at your kitchen island.

- Paint a picnic table a bright color and use it for your dining table.

- Surprise someone you love: order fresh Maine lobster and ship it to a friend.

- Install painted beadboard in your kitchen for charm and texture.

- Create your own "family specialty" version of fish chowder.

SALTWATER NEARBY 27

AN OCEAN INN

Grey Havens Inn
Hilda Hardcastle, Bill and Haley Eberhart

In the spring of 1976, after an intensive six-year search, Haley Eberhart's parents, the Hardcastles, bought this lovely old place, and with the help of their five children became Maine innkeepers.

Bill Eberhart, a son-in-law of the Hardcastles' now firmly rooted there himself, enjoys recalling the inn's rich family history. "In the early years, the Hardcastles would cheer up their overwhelmed children with the promise that if they would work hard and help pay the bills, they could one day turn the whole place into a five-family summer home, leave the beds unmade, and snooze on the porch from morning till night."

He laughs, "Porchloads of grandchildren later, that restful day is still receding into the future. But the promise worked on one generation, and Haley and I are already using it on our children."

Grey Havens is an easy-going, unpretentious place. Their view of tiny Five Islands Harbor is the best around. So are their trademark breakfast muffins, "Blueberries-barely-held-together-by-a-thin-coating-of-batter," the best in the world.

Hilda remembers, "In 1969 we came to Maine for the first time and rented a cottage on Capitol Island. I think we all knew immediately we'd be coming back as long as we lived. For the next six years we returned to that same cottage. The only things that bothered me were not having a place for a garden and not having anything for the kids to do.

"There was a small bed-and-breakfast on that island—something I'd never seen in Texas but had read about in English mysteries. It struck me that a small B & B was the perfect answer to both problems.

"So I spent the next five summers talking to realtors and traveling the coast and islands—Vinalhaven, Northhaven, Monhegan, Blue Hill, Northport—looking for a suitable property for my family. I finally found it just ten minutes by boat from Capitol Island."

Opened in June of 1904, the inn was called the Seguinland, after the Seguin Island Light. Seguin is a Native American word to describe the severe turbulence where the Kennebec River meets the Atlantic Ocean; "place where the ocean vomits" is the correct translation. Walter Reid, a businessman from Waterville, Maine, who at one point owned Mack Truck, steamships, and some real estate interests, built the sprawling inn for his friends. Another parcel of his estate, which he later gave to the state of Maine, is now known as Reid State Park, a favorite of summertime visitors.

Before the Hardcastles found the inn, many people had tried to revive it and failed. Once known by the locals as Heartbreak Hotel, the inn is believed to be one of the few classic shingle-style hotels still in operation on the Maine coast.

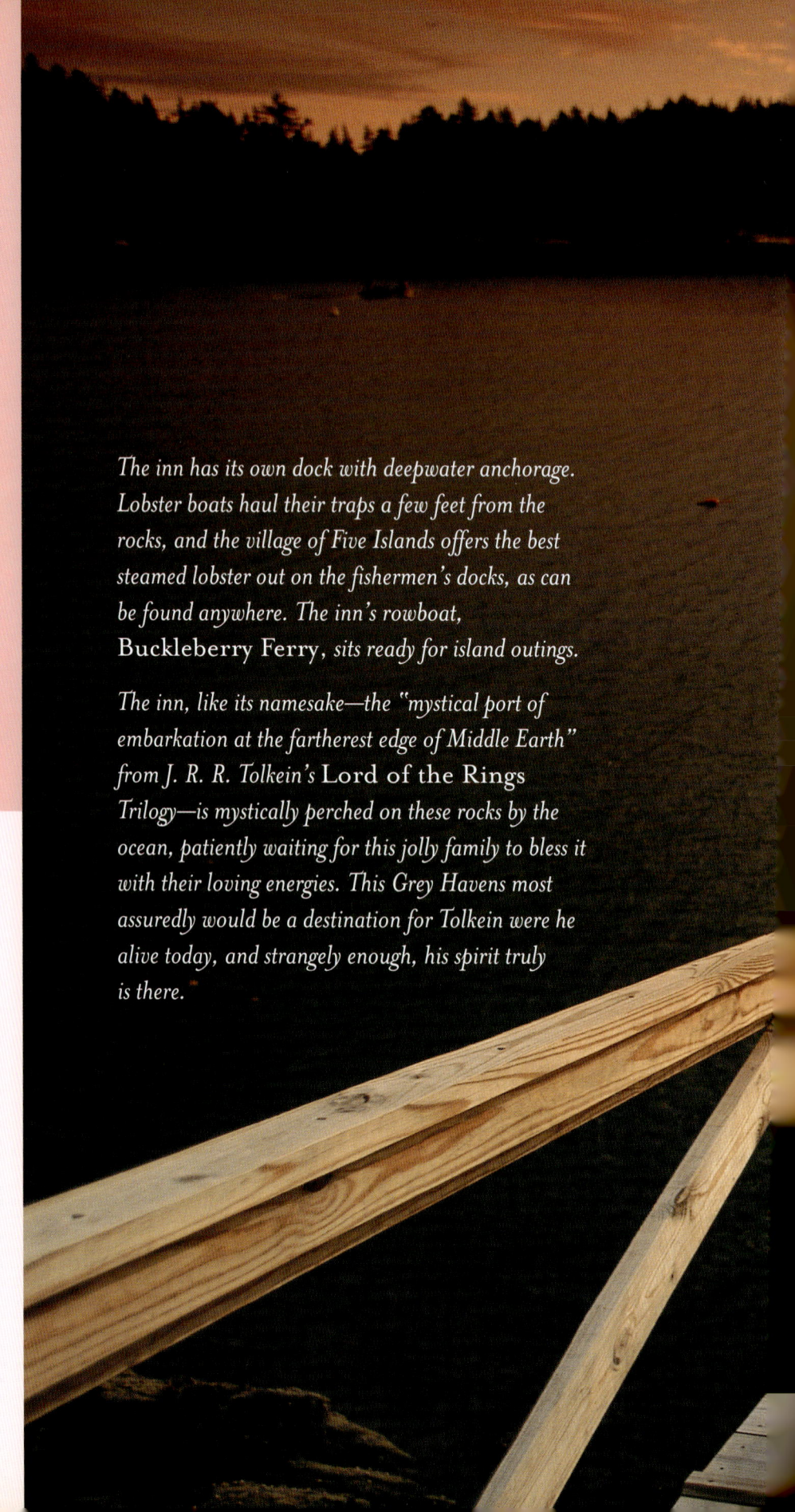

Previous Page: The big porch, half of it screened, wraps the inn on three sides. Its astounding views of the Atlantic Ocean and the islands of Sheepscot Bay are the most beautiful on earth. The setting is the ideal site for wedding receptions, family reunions, and gatherings of any kind. Tables for forty can be placed on the porch and another thirty to sixty people can be accommodated in the remarkably roomy dining room.

The inn has its own dock with deepwater anchorage. Lobster boats haul their traps a few feet from the rocks, and the village of Five Islands offers the best steamed lobster out on the fishermen's docks, as can be found anywhere. The inn's rowboat, Buckleberry Ferry, *sits ready for island outings.*

The inn, like its namesake—the "mystical port of embarkation at the fartherest edge of Middle Earth" from J. R. R. Tolkein's Lord of the Rings Trilogy*—is mystically perched on these rocks by the ocean, patiently waiting for this jolly family to bless it with their loving energies. This Grey Havens most assuredly would be a destination for Tolkein were he alive today, and strangely enough, his spirit truly is there.*

This grand view of the living room, or lounge, boasts a magnificent ocean view all its own. The original twelve-foot picture window, which the sofa is facing, was brought down from Rockland on an ice barge. It was the largest piece of glass in the state of Maine in 1904. As though touched by a magic wand, the golden, early-morning October sun fills the room with shimmering light.

Most of the furnishings are antiques of the comfy "cottagy" sort. Hilda, the grand dame of this great family, had the time of her life gathering items for the inn. She recalls when she once bought five fine iron beds—some with brass trim, all with rails in perfect shape—for a total of twenty-five dollars.

During that time, little painted tables were fifty cents each, and marseillaise counterpanes a dollar each at local thrift shops. Within five years, the boomers were furnishing their houses and apartments and the cost of these items went sky high.

Hilda and a friend discovered a pair of the little blue-painted iron daybeds in rural Maine back in the late '70s, and each went home with one. Hilda laughs to remember the countless times she has looked in the lounge to see a man (always the men) sound asleep on that daybed.

AN OCEAN INN 33

Above: A bath across the hall is papered with old sheet music. The sink is a reproduction, perfect for the space.

Right: Room number three, the east-corner turret room, is one of the few the family painted. The white, metal headboard was rescued from the cellar.

Above: A boatload of old wooden lobster buoys, discarded for the easier styrofoam ones, serves as the best vernacular lawn ornament in Maine. A spectacular autumn sun rises over the last day of another successful season at Grey Havens.

BRING MAINE HOME

- Find a local potter and order a custom set of dishes or mugs.

- Purchase quilts at a local bazaar to add color and spirit to your home.

- Use an antique basket to hold towels in the bath, or as a centerpiece, mounded with shells or pinecones you've collected.

- Make a simple curtain from vintage cloth for your kitchen or bath.

- Host an inexpensive wedding in your backyard or out in the pasture, with fresh-picked wildflowers and steamed lobsters.

AN OCEAN INN   35

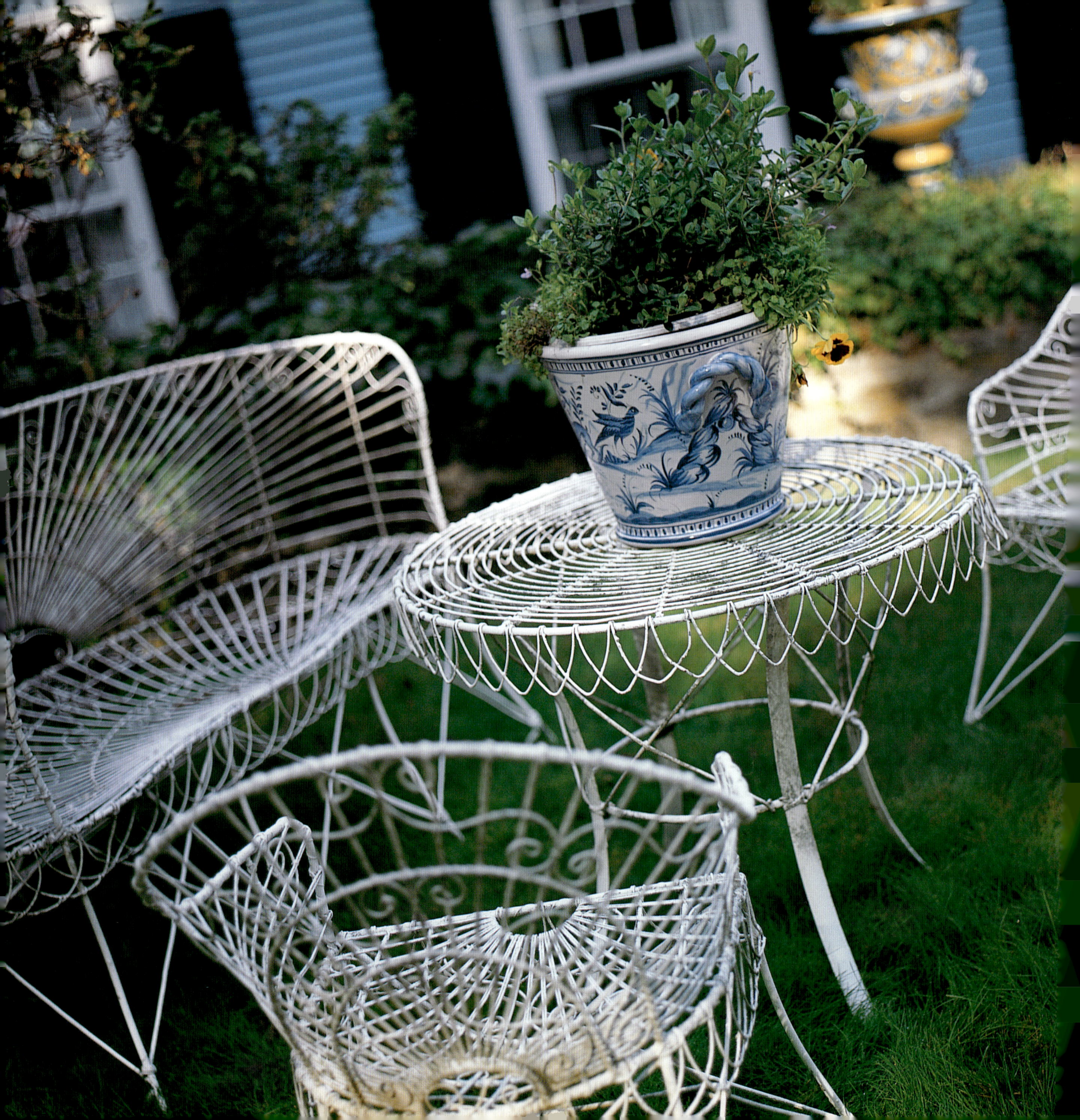

AN ISLAND SUMMER

Islesboro Summer House

For Brita Bonechi, Maine has always meant home. "Maine holds a profound beauty for me. Every fall of my childhood when we got in the car to leave for the winter, I felt as bereft as an outcast."

She asks, "What is it about this forceful, sometimes empty, and rugged landscape filled with elegant surprises that captivates me more than a peopled landscape? I think that part of it must be the thought that I really could discover something no one has ever seen or noted before. I might, for instance, be the first person to witness a bald eagle attacking sea ducks, be mobbed and chased off by terns. Or, more simply, I can watch the sun hitting ripples of a high tide."

It's the contradiction of Maine's grand beauty being captured in details, that she loves. "In Maine, any turn in the road brings a possibility to encounter overwhelming beauty. From the microcosms in a tidal pool to the sweep of Mt. Katahdin, all things rivet and require your attention."

For Bonechi, grand and beautiful details are as important inside her home as outside it. "My interior landscape is an extension of the outside . I am lucky in my house, because the light from the high tides of the harbor runs in reflected ripples up the walls and dances across the ceilings. That's the time when I feel the house really is not an imposition on the land but a glory.

"Although my house is a confusion of influences and passions, I choose clear colors that reflect the world outside. I choose objects that grip me with their beauty, ones that I could not bear the thought of never seeing again. We keep our family history alive by honoring our ancestors in photographs and paintings. This is what makes a home: the past and a family's presence."

Brita has spent every summer since she was eight days old at her family's home on Islesboro in Penobscot Bay. "Coming round the last curve down the driveway is coming home. A sense of relief and joy fills me. The dogs bark with sheer pleasure from the back of the car."

Most grand summer homes on the Maine Coast were large, shingle structures, but Brita's grandfather, William M. Elkins, wanted a New England–style farmhouse. He created Long Ledge in the 1940s and named it after the rock ledge the family could see during low tide. "Philanthropic Bill," as he was adoringly called, was a strong force in the creation of United Way. William L. Elkins, his father, was a robber baron. Their combined art collections contributed to the foundation of the Philadelphia Museum of Art. Brita chuckles that her grandmother was known in the family and in social circles as the "First of the Great Neurotics."

Long Ledge, in its early years, was aquamarine with white shutters. Each successive painting project, however, has evolved into a clear sky blue. Brita had the shutters painted black to moor the structure to its rocky landscape.

Eighteen years ago, Brita's mother, wishing to give the home an Italianate touch, had the sweet-smelling cedars *(Thuya occidentalis)* planted around the front entrance. They replaced the tired pink climbing roses that had struggled through decades of winter freezes.

38   MAINE LIVING

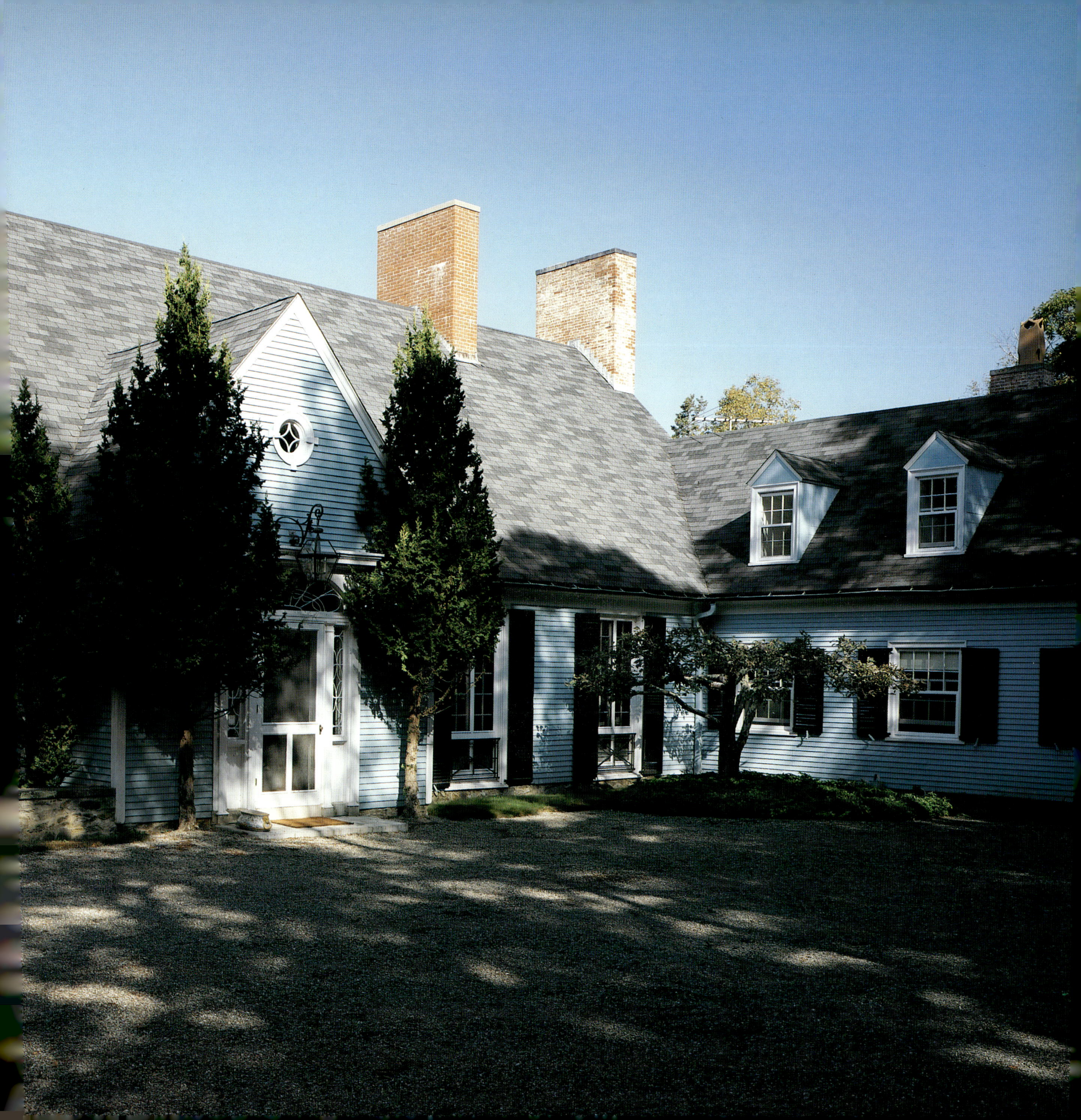

This blue and white bedroom has been Brita's since childhood. "The window seat has a box under it. In that box were my things, every year. Bill Ding was one of those things—a wooden man you put into acrobatic stances. Other things were pine and balsam pillows, books, drawing paper, and crayons. I would sit there and listen to grown-up parties downstairs on the porch. I sat there when my heart was broken. I sat there when I knew we were going to have our daughter Lilias. I sat there to draw when Lilias was tiny and napping. Sitting there I have seen the moon set over pink mountains in the fall. I have heard sea birds calling in the night and crows in the morning. I have seen ships and tankers and heard Gilkey's Bell clank and the foghorns moan."

Above: "The kitchen has always been where I've wanted to be unless I was on the porch or in a boat," says Brita.

Left: Tucked around the corner from the kitchen is a tiny, bright bathroom. Back in 1952, a cousin of Brita's became engaged to a cousin of the Rockefellers. Brita's mother was hosting an affair in celebration of the marriage. Anticipating Nelson and Happy Rockefeller as guests, she painted the floor a shimmering Chinese red. The red floor and buttery yellow wainscoting have been a happy combination ever since. The marble shelf above the sink holds Brita's silver bowls—prizes from sailing races.

AN ISLAND SUMMER 41

Above: Cecelia Donellen, who worked for the family and was Brita's close friend her entire childhood, lived in this room. When she retired, it became Carl Peter's room, a nephew of Brita's. Back then it had a little single bed in it and no chaise longue. The clear, pale-green-and-rose forms, and the white painted table, glow in the filtered light. Everything is settled and anchored to the dark floor in a restful composition that speaks from another era. The glass bottle's blue touch invigorates the space.

Above: The big sitting room is an "after-supper, rainy-night, game-playing room, and the fire must be lit! Otherwise it's very large and dark," says Brita. The red lamps and the pair of red ceramic poppies, made by artist-friend Sharon Townsend, perk up the space as only red can. The sky-blue sofa has been there as long as Brita can remember. Brita's garden painting on the mantel echoes her bighearted bouquet behind the sofa.

Left: During the war years of the 1940s, when even the well-to-do had to make do, small touches from the raucous Roaring Twenties were mixed in with the more tailored style of the era, an effort to create a look of luxury. A marbleized checkerboard was painted on the diagonal entry floorboards rather than tiled with real marble. Twin gentle wing chairs, slipcovered with curtains from the grandparents' Philadelphia house, still sit where they were originally positioned.

Left: Roberto's father restored the old metal bed. Years ago in Italy, when people moved from their farms to the cities, they frequently abandoned the belongings they could not carry by the side of the road. Roberto's father would find these wonderful beds and refinish them.

The fanciful quilt of colorful postage-sized squares was made on the island and bought from the Second Baptist Church Sewing Circle by Brita's mother forty years ago.

Paintings by Brita and artist friend Robert Shetterly hang above a classic white-painted end table.

"The hall outside my door is dangerous and dark and should be rushed through. After forty years of this, I am getting over it, but I still lock my door at night, as the latch doesn't work properly and the door can swing open with a draft. There are bat stories."

AN ISLAND SUMMER 45

This second-floor hallway glows in the morning light. Tucked over the kitchen wing, the hall leads to two guest bedrooms and a roomy linen closet. A journey up to the hall usually leaves Brita wondering how the dogs got there and left leaves on the floor.

46   MAINE LIVING

The essence of summer: an afternoon southerly blows warmly through an upstairs room.

AN ISLAND SUMMER

Summer Flowers

Maine's clear skies and crisp, salty air, coastal fog, and cool-to-moderate temperatures create the perfect environment for an abundance of wildflowers and perennials. Throughout the summer season and into the fall, roadsides and pastures are sprinkled with radiant blooms.

In late spring the ladyslippers start the blooming parade, while Memorial Day ushers in fragrant lilacs. Mid-June brings fields full of spiked lupines, and the seasons continue with daisies, then dandelions, lilies, black-eyed Susans, loosestrife, fireweed, chicory, and, finally, autumn's asters bringing up the rear. Years ago, when the climate was cooler, the parade was considerably more drawn out. With today's warmer climate, flowers rush by breathlessly like their human earth-mates, scurrying to live before the season ends.

Lilacs by the barn.

Top Left: One of August's wine-colored poppies.

Top Right: Daisies with morning glories.

Bottom Left: Buttery-yellow daylilies kissed with dew.

Bottom Right: Bold, showy poppies meet subtle lavender irises.

AN ISLAND SUMMER 49

BRING MAINE HOME

- Paint a bedroom or bathroom floor with a bright, shiny enamel.

- Instead of buying flowers, choose something from outside; even bare branches can be beautiful.

- Use more red or magenta: small touches—a cushion, a vase—create powerful focal points.

- Make a date to play Scrabble or double solitaire on Wednesday evenings.

- Create a window seat in front of your best view and use it often.

Top Left: A midsummer bouquet of blue hydrangea.

Top Right: Sweetpeas create a beautiful welcome at a home's entrance.

Bottom Left: Autumn joy sedum brings a festival of colors.

Bottom Right: Elegant and delicate engineering: poppy seed-globes.

Maine Living

Wild lupines in a field by the shore.

Simple Structures

Sheds, Shacks, and Cabins

Tiny sheds remind us of children's drawings, or of our own drawings when we were in nursery school and the teacher asked us to draw our house; they are primitive, naïve, elementary, charming.

Remember the structures you made with a box of blocks? No architect, no builder, no interior designer—just you. Two hands joined at the fingertips in a tent-like shape is the gesture for house in sign language. Four walls and an A-frame roof: this comfortable, safe, familiar, and secure shape offers the simplest of shelters, all we need for survival.

In shape, form, and color, we are our houses. When we look at a shed, a cabin, an outbuilding, that structure is us, pared down to our simplest forms—our heart and soul embodied. These little boxes contain our spirits.

The Maine landscape is alive with vernacular architecture—sheds, shacks, barns, garages, cabins, workshops. The coast is encrusted with little waterfront and wharf buildings—bait shacks, boathouses, repair sheds, boxy little pitched-roof and shed-roofed structures where fishermen store and repair their nets, traps and buoys.

They grow naturally and unselfconsciously, like wooden barnacles.

Inland, these elementary Maine structures serve as outhouses, icehouses, ice-fishing shanties, pump houses, warming huts, farm stands, and, in expanded form, potato barns, hunting camps, and tourist cabins.

What all of these Maine structures have in common is that they are modest, handmade, and made of wood, Maine being the most heavily wooded state in the union. They are purely functional; their form is derived from their utility and their aesthetic arises from the uses to which they are put and the people who use them. Basic and sturdy, they are built to withstand a cold, wet environment. They are wonderfully weathered, sometimes sagging under the weight of a lifetime of snow. But they are authentic and they are sufficient.

All too often these days, the charming, wooden idiosyncrasy of the real Maine shed is replaced by the bland sameness of manufactured sheds—tinny, mass-produced, and soulless. Worse still, the repetitive roadside eyesores of rent-a-shed storage complexes. That is why we must celebrate the wonderful humility of the home-made, the hut, the shack, the cabin, the home that we designed for ourselves when we were but children. All children are artists. All shacks are art.

Above: Maine is famous for its little "overnight tourist boxes" all up and down the coast, near ponds and rivers. Some have been here since the early 1900's and people enjoy their intimate and cozy qualities that are nonexistent in a modern motel. Guests are usually people from nearby eastern seaboard states; guests of a local wedding, writers looking for a room of one's own, hikers, and fishermen.

Cabins are moderately priced and an elegant step up from a rustic night lying on the ground in a tent. They are revered for their historical place in Maine vacationland tradition. They have refused to step aside for the construction of more "modern" motels. People make plans to meet friends annually in these small guest quarters. They have the same social flare and easygoing friendliness found in campgrounds. Some even have their own tiny fireplaces.

Below: The North Whitefield volunteer fire department was organized in 1944. When there is a fire in the area the alarm rings in three towns; North Whitefield, Whitefield, and Cooper's Mills, and the firemen decide who goes where. The light on this October day makes the raspberry doors sparkle at this crossroad. The intense blue sky above makes a composition of clear colors and forms that inspires like a poem.

Simple Structures 55

This ramshackle house sits on a sandy beach that stretches out to a working harbor filled with fishing boats and lobster boats.

Above: Everyone needs a personal shed for their stuff. This tiny building up in Cobscook Bay reflects the forests and ocean nearby; cedar shingles and aqua trim. When most people have gone back to their winter homes, this shelter stands guard storing rakes, shovels, bird feeders, and garden stakes over long winter months.

Below: In 1932 Louis Marstaller's father had eight cabins constructed on a wooded piece of land overlooking a small cattail-filled pond. Today twenty cabins make up The Maine Idyll Motor Court, "cottages among the trees." The humble cabins have modernized kitchenettes, but repairs have been minimal and well within the boundaries of their grandfather's original concept. The stone fireplaces, all original, have an artist's flare in their compositions. Subtle paintings and poems from family members are hung here and there on the pine-paneled walls.

Below: Julian, age five, plays outside what was once the summer kitchen of the old Davis farm, the first structure on this mid-coastal peninsula. The Davis farm at one time was used as guest quarters for parents of children attending a camp on Crotch Island across from the peninsula. Today it's still the kitchen and still has no insulation. The fog and wind constantly slip between the boards of the structure; even the light shines through the cracks. The wood cookstove in the kitchen must be fired up constantly.

SIMPLE STRUCTURES

The house of this old farm burned many years ago, but the barns were saved. A new wave of back-to-the-landers are beginning to create small working organic farms, bringing new life to the countryside.

BRING MAINE HOME

- Build your own potting shed.

- Rescue a beautiful old structure from demolition and move it to your backyard.

- If you can't rescue it, salvage its beautiful wood or metal fixtures.

- Design your new home to be a series of small, connected outbuildings instead of a single large, boxy one.

- Join your local historical society.

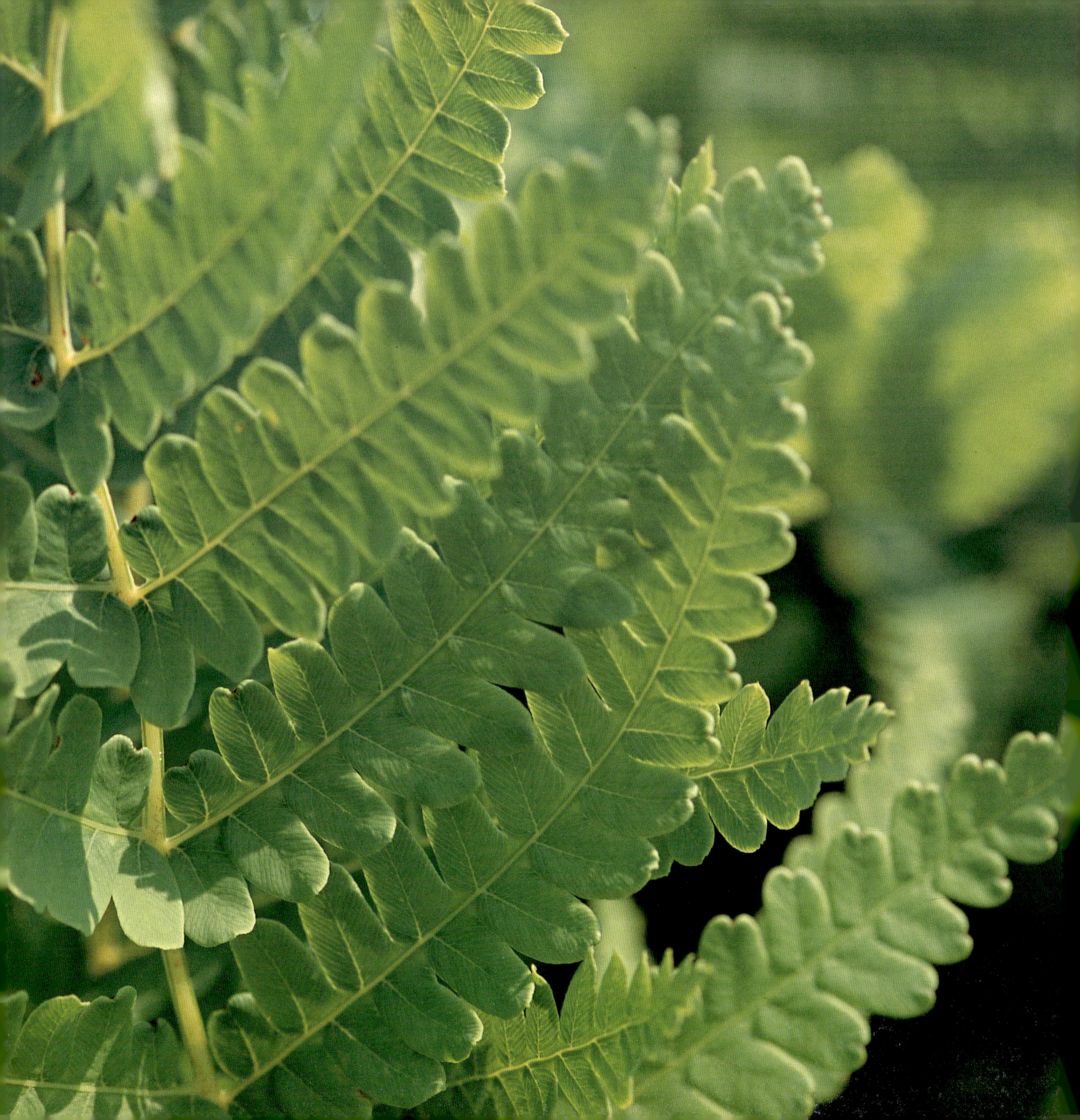

PASSIONATE WORK, PASSIONATE PEOPLE

Belle of Maine

Belle of Maine Canning Company, founded in 1898 in Wilton, Maine, is a spunky, low-tech business that's refused to fold, while most manufacturing businesses in Maine vamoosed overseas long ago.

Poet David Whyte speaks of the importance of keeping a well-traveled cow path next to the "information highway." Butch Wells Jr. and his father, Adrian "Butch" Sr., tend that cow path by canning baked beans, fiddleheads (still-unfurled ferns), and dandelion greens, just the way great-grandfather W. S. Wells did. They plant and harvest the beans and greens they preserve, hiring family and friends as employees and making their schedules flexible enough to pick up kids from school.

Nestled in the mountains of western Maine, the village of Wilton sits around the southeastern shores of Wilson Pond—"A great place to live, to work, to play," as all the signs proclaim as you travel into town.

A mile up the hill from Main Street, right across from the road to Wilson Pond, sits the canning shop, spinning like a marvelous giant toy.

On a sunny April morning, the wide doors open to reveal machinery that whines and whirls. Butch Sr.'s prize tulips that grow between his house and the shop immediately describe a man with a golden heart. He says, "There were times when we didn't have a dollar for a loaf of bread, but we always found money for flowers."

Right: Fiddlehead foragers unload bushel bags of the tender green curls at the shop's side door throughout the spring. Butch empties the greens into measured crates.

Below: Butch Jr. and Butch Sr. stand in the doorway of Belle of Maine.

Above, Left: The fern tips are loaded into perforated metal drums fashioned from the rims of Model A wheels. They spin slowly while antique fans blow the chaff from the spinning green tips.

Passionate Work, Passionate People   65

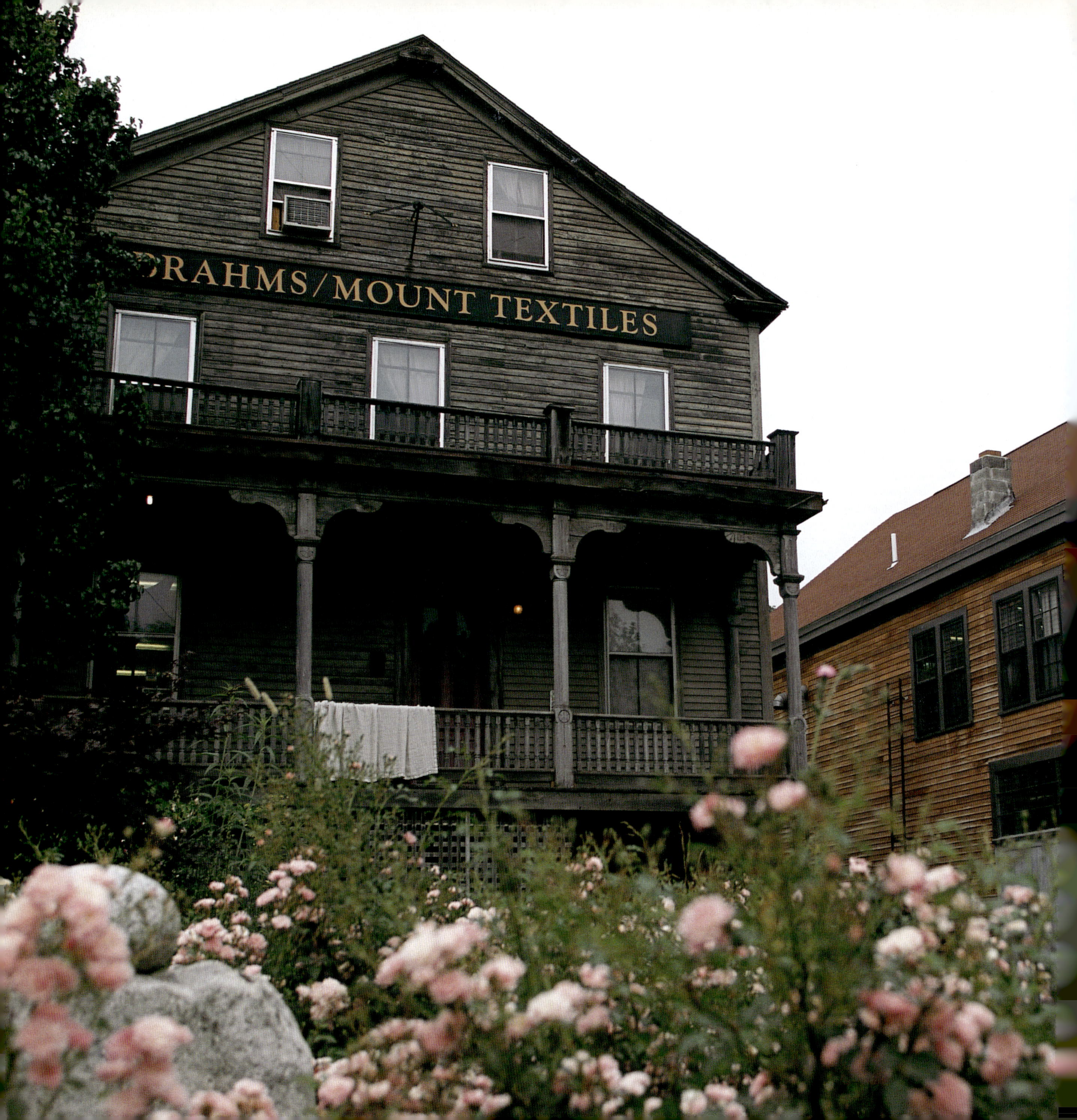
BRAHMS/MOUNT TEXTILES

PASSIONATE WORK, PASSIONATE PEOPLE

Brahms/Mount Textiles

Claudia Brahms and Noel Mount founded their textile company in 1983. Compared to Belle of Maine, Brahms/Mount is a young business. But it possesses the same impressive qualities of the canning company: it's small, focused, and family run. The products are made in-house, and feel and smell as pure as summertime in Maine.

Noel and Claudia met in Greenville, Maine—a story that was just meant to be:

"We both grew up in textile families in very different parts of the world, and ended up working together at Guilford of Maine, a major textile industry; I worked in textile design, and Noel redesigned the mill for streamlined manufacturing," Claudia says.

"Our adventure together began with our love and commitment to the manufacturing process and the preservation of fine craftsmanship. After a long and wonderful day riding motorcycles around Maine, searching for a place to start our business, we parked in Hallowell, a town we had driven through but never stopped at before. While having coffee at Slates Restaurant, we heard about two historic buildings that once housed the Hallowell Granite Company." The rest, as they say, is history.

Noel rescued several ancient shuttle looms from defunct textile mills around Maine. He began the process of rebuilding the looms and the rambling, ancient buildings that now house their manufacturing, offices, and living quarters, where they design and weave natural fiber cotton and linen blankets that are manufactured with impeccable attention to quality, craftsmanship, and beauty.

Top Left: When Kenny, a friend of Claudia and Noel's, plays at the coffee shop in town, he sometimes comes early and stops by the office. Claudia and Noel say that welcoming the unexpected is vital to their designing, their success, their mantra, their philosophy of life. So Kenny's visit is the perfect kind of stimulation and serendipity on which they thrive.

Above, Left: The elegant, practical, linen and cotton blankets are named for beautiful places in Maine; Monhegan, Stonington, Bristol.

The colors are inspired by Maine's natural beauty; moss, lichen, granite, bird nests, cedar branches, deep blue water, daylilies.

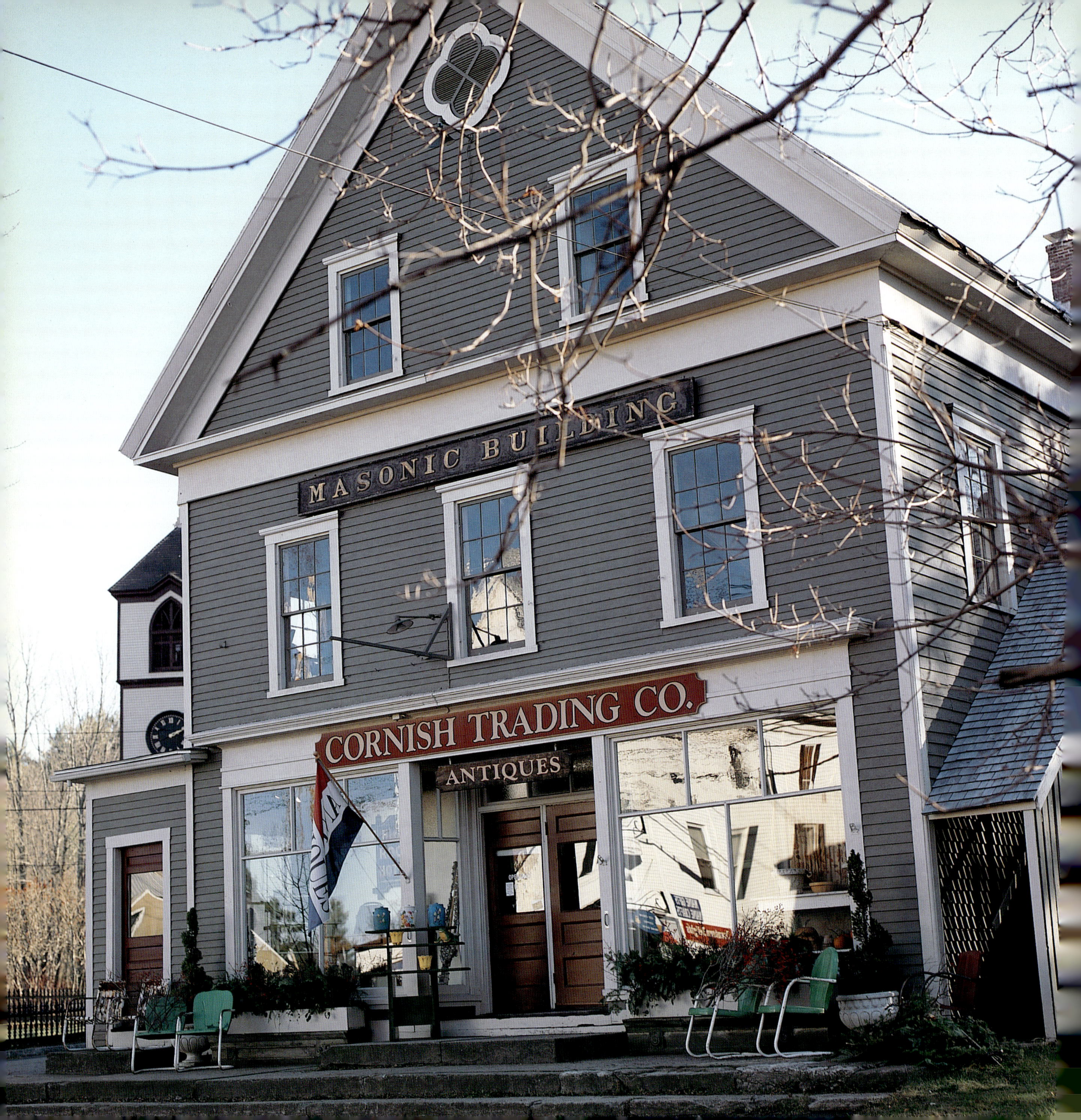
MASONIC BUILDING
CORNISH TRADING CO.
ANTIQUES

PASSIONATE WORK, PASSIONATE PEOPLE

Cornish Trading Company

Cornish is among those hundreds of gems of small towns in Maine that are off the beaten track, charming and well worth discovering. Main Street is sprinkled with homey antiques stores, inns, and tiny restaurants. The small village is nestled on a path the Almouchiquois Native Americans used during the 1600s. Back then it was the Pequawket Trail, the "Sandy Land" Trail that connected Biddeford Pool on the Atlantic Coast to the Mt. Washington Valley of New Hampshire's White Mountains.

Located near where the Ossipee River joins the Saco River, Cornish hosts yearly strawberry festivals, apple festivals, and down-home bluegrass festivals.

Owner Francine O'Donnell and her mother, Ceci O'Donnell, light up the town with their friendliness and humor. Francine owns one of the state's most adventurous and exciting antiques businesses, representing around thirty-five top-quality dealers.

Above: A sampling of the Cornish Trading Company's wares. Francine says, "The shop opens for the season April 1 with a wild following of people from all over the country. The line typically snakes around the parking lot and down the side of the building. My dealers buy and stash all winter in preparation for the event. They really go all out with newly picked merchandise, creative displays, and fresh flowers. My mother, Ceci, works with me and we always have fun! I do send invitations to folks on our ever-growing mailing list, but many of the loyal following mark their calendars well in advance."

Right: Built in 1865, the charming old shop once housed the village's general store and post office and now retains most of its original architectural features.

72 MAINE LIVING

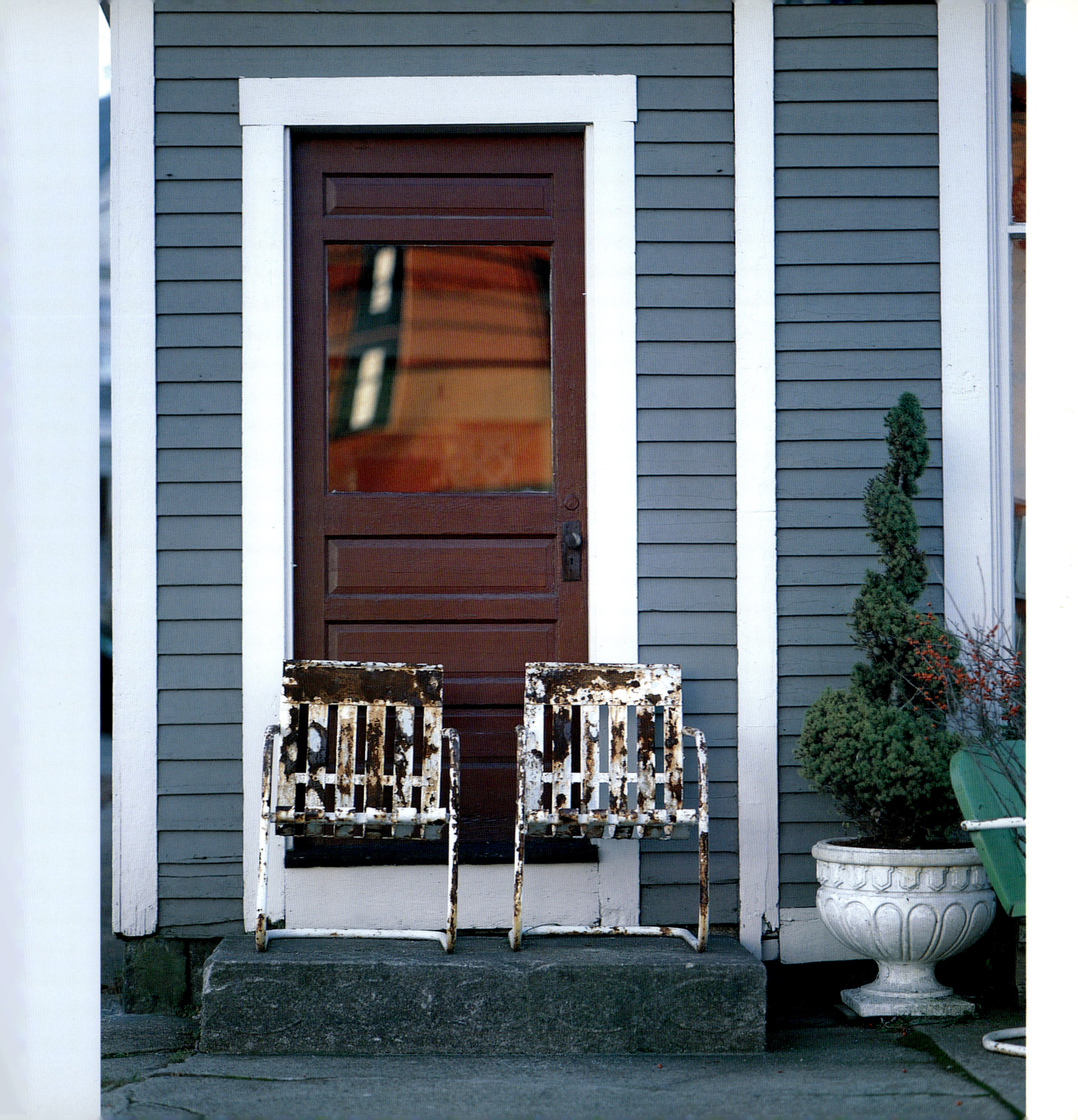

PASSIONATE WORK, PASSIONATE PEOPLE

Fish Monger

Alvin Dennison is the man behind the colorful truck on Route 1 near Thomaston. He has been selling fish by the side of the road since the early 1990s. He enjoys talking with his regular customers and seeing the same summer folks return year after year.

He was born in South Thomaston and currently lives in Owl's Head, Maine. He served in the Army and is a Vietnam vet. He painted his truck in patriotic colors and sends pictures to various local residents serving in Iraq. He says that when he was in the Army, he would have loved familiar sites from home.

A ten-speed bike and an exercise machine that he found at a yard sale are kept back in the woods for times when business is slow.

OUR CAUSE WAS JUST
QUEST
FOOD STAMPS
CLAMS
300
SMOKED
TROUT
SALMON
LOBSTER
MEAT
HAKE 4 25
SHRIMP
MEAT 6 50
SCALLOPS
6.75
HADDOCK
GOD BLESS AMERICA
CRABMEAT
CLAMS
6 00
5 75
3 00
MUSSELS
1 00
SMOKED TROUT
SCALLOPS 675
PROUD AMERICAN
LOBSTER
7.25
465
FINANHADIE 650
BACK OFF
LANDLUBBER!!
MAINE
9874

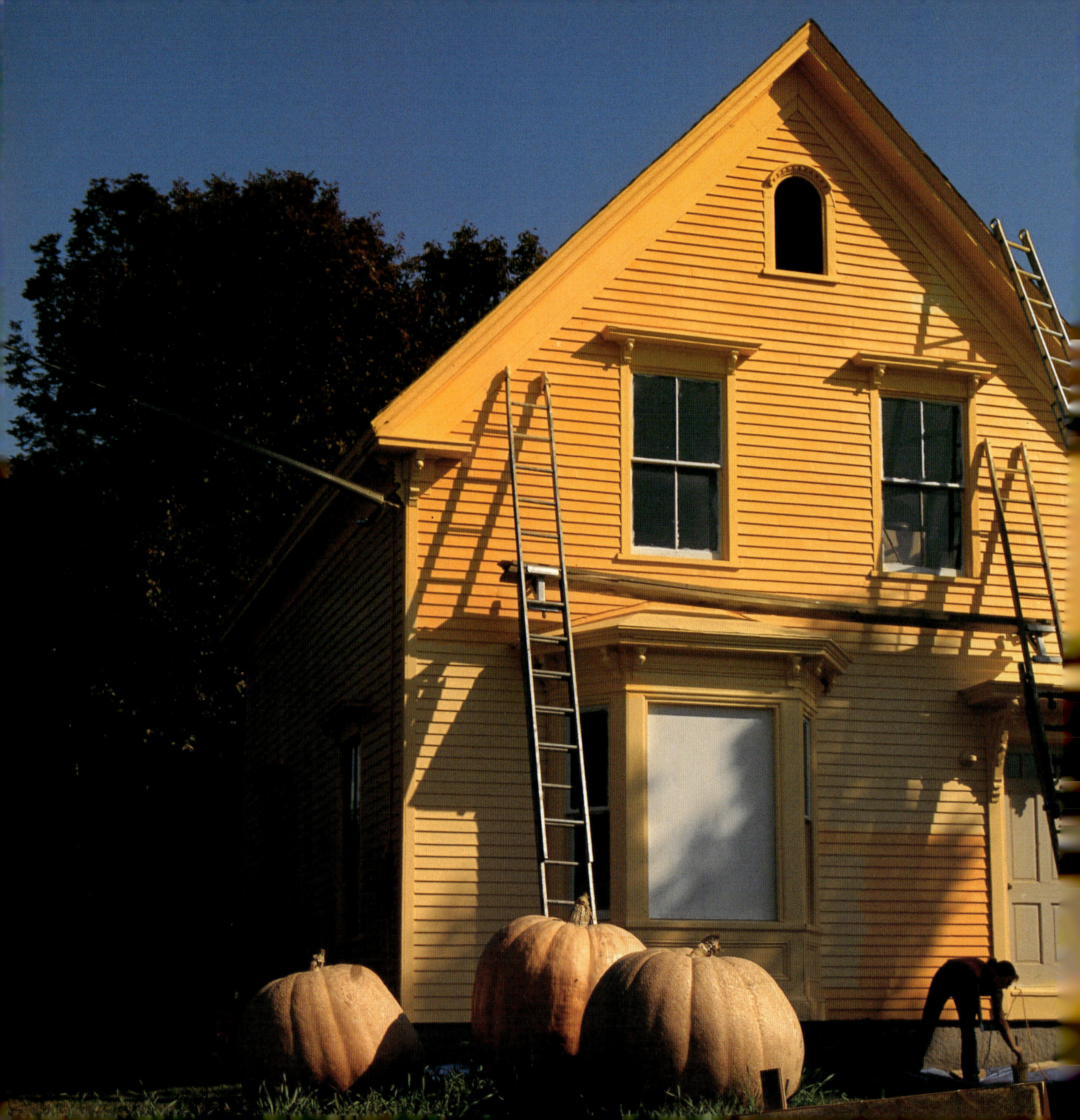

PASSIONATE WORK, PASSIONATE PEOPLE

A Photographer's Workshop

This bright-yellow house belongs to William Wheeler Anderson, a professional photographer.

Located on Route 1 near Camden, Maine, the bold color stands out amidst the familiar white of the colonial homes farther down the road.

The air and space in Maine have always encouraged individual expression.

PORT CLYDE GENERAL STORE
NO PARKING
We Sell and Install Quality
DOUGLAS BATTERIES
UNLEADED PLUS

PASSIONATE WORK, PASSIONATE PEOPLE

Port Clyde General Store

Port Clyde is the archetypal Maine coastal fishing village. Everything one could dream of surrounds you there, like a merry-go-round of sites, sounds, and smells: a ferryboat to the islands, a harbor chock-full of lobster and fishing boats, hundreds of seagulls, a tiny seafood shack out on the dock, a boatyard and marina, an art gallery, an old inn. There are a few sunny days in the summer, but Port Clyde's winds bring fog that lingers for great swipes of the summer.

The General Store, so typical of hundreds of general stores still thriving in Maine, offers staples, sundries, and homemade treats. The most beautiful and delectable cinnamon buns ever are placed out on the counters at six-thirty each morning.

The store, with old wooden floors and wooden shelves—wooden everything—rambles near the docks. It's a spirited place for locals and visitors alike, welcoming and life-affirming after malls and malls of steel and plastic.

82   MAINE LIVING

PASSIONATE WORK, PASSIONATE PEOPLE

Jim Blankman Woodworking

Jim Blankman, woodworker of Eastport, works with "whatever comes along." Right now he's building kitchen cabinets. Tomorrow it may be recreating old colonial molding in a house down the street. His real passion is the teardrop trailers he builds for his clients. They are designed to hook up to antique woodies, but he's made many for regular modern vehicles.

His last client was a Kentucky outdoorsman who wanted a camper to extend his fishing and hunting season.

Jim can be found in his shop at the end of Main Street in Eastport.

Passionate Work, Passionate People

Antique Tractors

In the village of Lovell on a curve in the road sits the Lovell Garage, operated by Don Chandler for over forty years. Three mechanics work on cars, light trucks, and farm equipment the year through. They also sell tires and used farm equipment, along with antique tractors.

The sun setting on antique tractors out front creates an improvised outdoor museum of mechanical wonders.

BRING MAINE HOME

- Paint your house a cheerful yellow.

- Try adding your own dandelion greens to a sandwich.

- Learn who the painting professors are at your local university and purchase an original painting for your office or home.

- Create an eclectic interior by placing beautiful primitive pieces from your favorite antique shop in a sleek, modern setting.

- Use old, metal garden chairs lined with cushions around your supper table.

- Choose blankets and throws of natural fibers—wool, linen, and cotton—for your beds

PASSIONATE WORK, PASSIONATE PEOPLE 85

RURAL LANDSCAPES

Art and Antiques

Union, Maine, settled in 1774, is located on the St. George River about ten miles from the coast. With only two thousand residents, the town is quiet and very neighborly, traits that are reflected in the rolling farmland spread out around Seven Tree Pond and Round Pond. It's the town that Ben Ames Williams, the American novelist and short-story writer, made famous in his historical novel *Come Spring,* published in 1940.

Brian White purchased this 1789 Cape Cod cottage in Union back a few years as a place to show and sell his antiques. But he quickly realized that scouring the state for antiques was more thrilling than waiting for customers, so Brian, his wife Lynne, and their four children—Joel, Tiffany, Eben, and Orchard—created their home here.

"The thing about Maine that I am in love with," says Brian, "is its expressiveness: the juxtapositions of the violent and the gentle; the Northeast winter winds and the still, quiet coastal fog. When I can spend several hours in a day walking the shoreline, emptying out and connecting to that wildness, that's where the charge is. That's where I pick up my energy."

You'll find him up early. "My favorite times of day are dawn and twilight—those in-between stages when a certain light unlike any other strikes the atmosphere."

Art has always been a part of Brian's life. Some of his most important lessons came from Maine's masters. "When I was nine years old I won an art contest at school that changed my life. We lived in Cushing, near the Wyeth family compound. My father was in the antiques business then, and Andrew Wyeth would come to the house to buy old frames for his paintings. Soon after that contest, on one of his visits, I asked him how I could be a painter. He said that what I must do is be a good observer."

As the details in his own artwork show now, that was a lesson he has taken to heart. "That awakening of the senses is what I am always aware of. It is what I always try to do—stay the observer. Maine has a beauty that continually awakens me."

Above: The colorful brush strokes of this stenciling transform the atmosphere of the living room and add a touch of formality. Back at the turn of the eighteenth century, one Moses Eaton and his son traveled the area, painting lively colors and forms on rural folks' plaster walls. People could not afford the European wallpaper that landed in Boston during those years. Moses created a vocation for himself and many others by peddling designs similar to the costly wallpaper. Many men shared this profession and often traded patterns with each other. Brian, inspired by patterns from Moses Eaton books, has created his own fanciful designs.

Right: Rugged, weathered, and solid, like himself, Brian's old house stands braced and wide open to the elements, to the main road, and to his clients: museum directors, gallery owners, and antiques dealers who depend on his eye to give life to their businesses.

Brian successfully weaves his two passions of art and antiques into his life's work. The two obsessions are perfect partners, nurturing and inspiring each other. His excitement over collections of old shells, old foghorns, even old buckets, fuels his art-making.

RURAL LANDSCAPES 89

90 MAINE LIVING

Left Page: On an early-morning walk several years ago, Brian collected a handful of mussel shells from the beach. He kept them for days in his pocket, bringing them out to marvel at their beauty. Handling the shells and meditating on his connection with the ocean, his times with his father on the beach, his love of the strong people who lived near the shore, their clothing, their stories—all these twirling thoughts synthesized into Brian's idea of the dress.

Brian gathered his kids for a trip to the shore to collect bags full of shells. The final phase was one of amazing engineering and the meticulous placing of hundreds of shells culminating in a sculpture of a female form bedazzled in shells. **Mussel Dress** *seems to be waiting backstage for a costume change by an actress performing in some watery opera.*

Below Right: The elaborate and elegant **Island Bride** *waits completion—a gown fashioned from cut pieces of shells that form rows of lace, embodying a dreamy concept of wistful femininity.*

Brian's shell sculptures exemplify the female form with a lustrous energy and appeal that recalls the intricate shell motifs created during the baroque period in Europe. In fact, the ocean and the baroque period—that period between the 1600s and the 1750s when monarchs employed artists and composers to out-create each other—are the sources of his inspiration.

Left: Two smaller, delicate female forms are works in progress.

RURAL LANDSCAPES 91

Above: A pair of wooden pins sit next to a yellow, vinegar-grained chest that dates to around 1830.

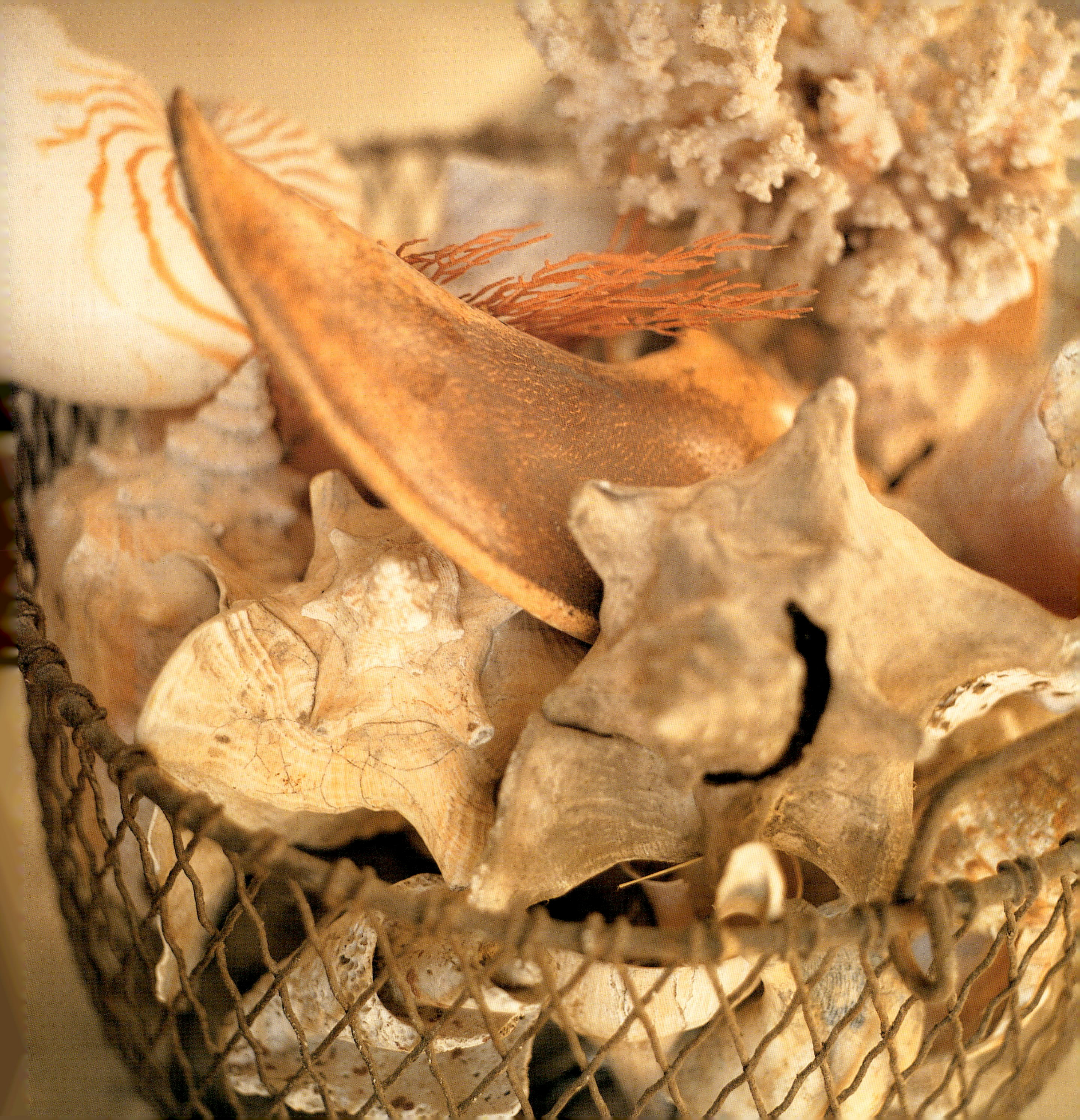

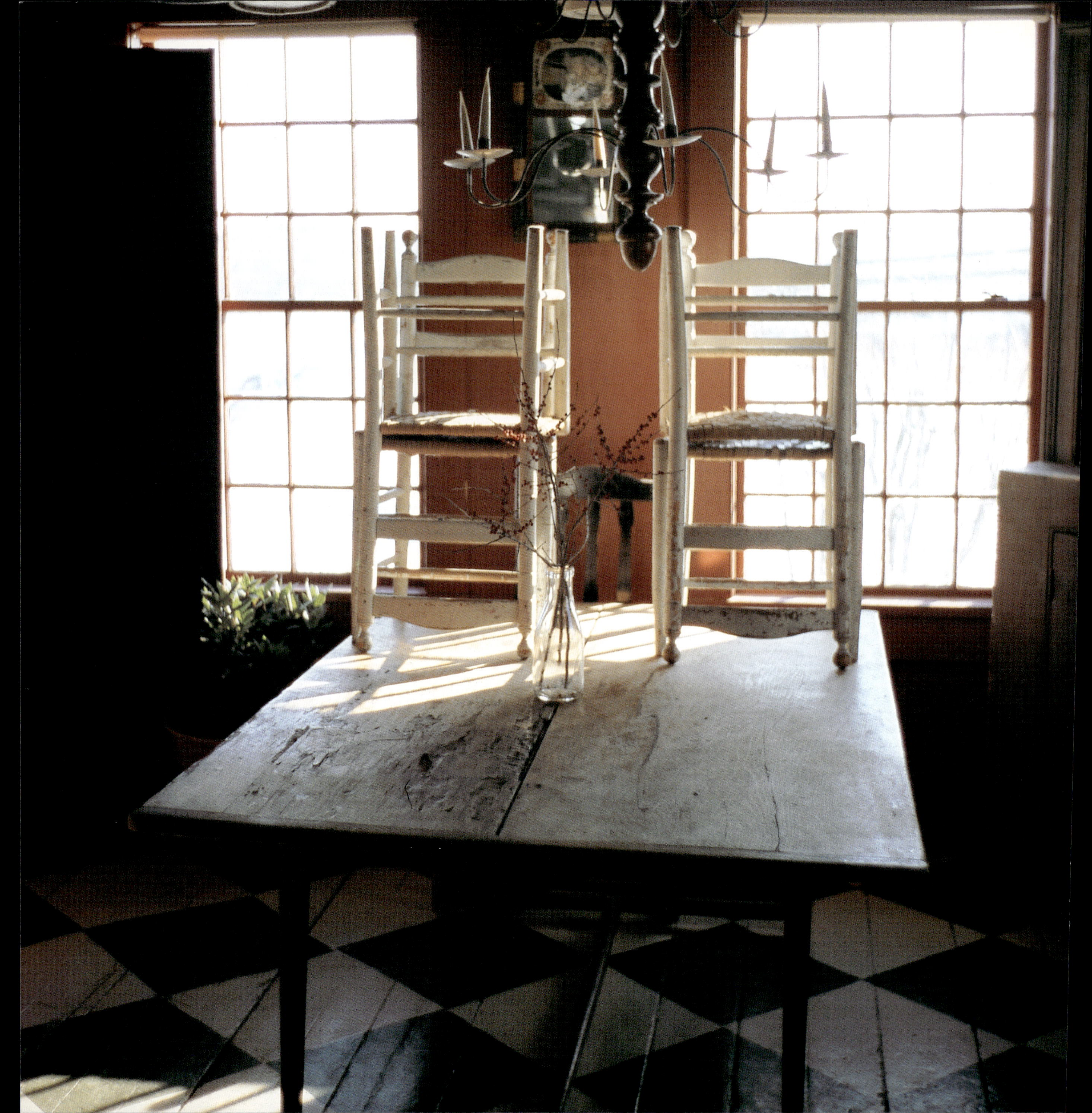

Left: The Whites have an antiques business that focuses on New England painted pieces. Their home is filled to the rafters with the favorites they've chosen to enjoy awhile.

The dining table, made from two twenty-four-inch boards, was found in an old barn in Whitefield. It was turned upside-down and had a pool of water on it from the leaky roof. It had probably been there in the same position for more than a hundred years.

Brian can't bear the thought of repairing the table so it stays, with the white-painted chairs on top most of the day until mealtime. The table's sculptural quality, with space flowing under it, somehow honors its long history in that barn.

With the chairs on the table, the cream-and-olive-painted checkerboard floor shows off. Round, painted barrels hang from the ceiling like giant checker pieces above a game board.

Above: Red berries in a milk bottle glow in the afternoon winter sun.

RURAL LANDSCAPES

Left: Entering the dining room, where colorful washtubs hang from the ceiling, you are reminded of a children's book about frogs falling from the sky. Maybe the buckets catch those frogs? Are they holding the silverware or keeping further drips from the table? The simple answer is that Brian loves their bright colors. He has kept their original colors the way he found them. When he would stop at people's homes to inquire about antiques, the washtubs were always around. He loves them as remnants of antique homes. He loves their simplicity and utilitarian spirit. He enjoys thinking about the people who washed their clothes in them. He even loves thinking about the clothes.

The rusty red of the vertical wide-board paneling was the predominant shade during the eighteenth century because the ingredients to create it were so readily available.

A thin black wash on the ceiling creates a strong graphic appeal, and a dramatic background for showing the buckets. The dark ceiling, like negative space, plays off the light of the floor, generating a low-level energy in the room.

Brian designed the woodstove and had a friend construct it. In Maine, practicality is as important as beauty, and though it might not appeal to some, the foil tacked on the wall serves as a perfect heat shield, one that doesn't trap the heat between the walls.

A mitten tree, an essential in all Maine homes, dries the children's gloves after each sledding spree.

Left: Brian's special starlike interpretation of a compass cheers up the small niche between the dining and living spaces. The compass icon often decorated old sea chests. The symbol was believed to keep evil spirits away on long sailing trips.

A simple settee holds several comfortable pillows made from the antique fabrics the Whites love to collect.

Below: "Cat" peeks around a cabinet in the kitchen, where the aromas of a roast and winter vegetables permeate the room.

RURAL LANDSCAPES 97

Above: A parade of old horns, another of Brian's fascinations, ushers guests from the mudroom into the kitchen. Kids played the red, white, and blue horns in Fourth of July celebrations. Other horns were used on small boats and dories on foggy days near the coast.

Right: On an old meetinghouse bench, two Fourth of July horns stand on the seat, and two framed, schoolgirl needlework pieces hang above, samplers by students learning the art of sewing. Two fruit studies balance the composition. Brian found the pastel of peaches and grapes, and he crafted the still life in the gold frame beneath it. The watermelon, pears, plums, and strawberries on an oval platter are all constructed from hundred-year-old fabric.

BRING MAINE HOME

- Find fresh uses for antique furniture—metal clam baskets or egg baskets for storage. Pull an old church pew next to the dining table. Use a sewing table as a bedside table.

- Paint old paneling an apple-red or fir-green.

- Give your old garden furniture a new lease on life: add weathered boards to its metal frame to remake it into a rustic dining table.

- Take a child antiquing and help them start a collection—old postcards, billiard balls—that they can enjoy for a lifetime.

- Use the floor as a canvas; paint it! Try a grass-green or a sky-blue for a bedroom, or a checkerboard pattern in a bathroom.

Above: Many of Brian's projects are placed throughout the house. One alluring theme is "the grand tour," when the country first experienced a rise in travel abroad. He collects old shoes and trunks, embellishing them with his own travel stories. The spirit of these women's pumps is boosted with layers of old Chinese currency and postage stamps.

RURAL LANDSCAPES 99

The porch's wicker rockers were the gift of a summer guest who found them at a neighbor's barn sale.

RURAL LANDSCAPES

Back to the Land

Paul and Dianne Schelble and their four children, ages nine, seven, five, and one year, came to Maine from Michigan in 1977 as part of the back-to-land movement that was sweeping the country.

Being in the middle of an energy crunch and having grown up in the '60s, they were searching, like everyone else at that time, for a way to live without consuming oil.

Dianne recounts, "For many years we lived without a television, without plumbing, and without central heat. Today, with grown children spread all about, we still enjoy our 'no TV' life. Plumbing arrived around 1986, and we waited until 1999 to install central heating. We turn up the heat only on the coldest of nights. We live comfortably in our 'coolness.' Our oldest son tells us he had to leave for college to enjoy some of life's basic comforts!"

For Paul and Dianne, life's comforts have been here in Maine for more than twenty-five years now. "Our home is right in the middle of our forty acres, and like many of our spread-out neighbors, we look straight to the horizon for our daily sunrise," Dianne says. "We still harvest our firewood from our own woodlot and find there is nothing as sweet as a roaring wood fire on a cold winter evening. The road from our house leads right into town, so we're not far from our neighbors, and we get together regularly."

Dianne admits that sometimes they have been caught with a shortage of funds, but "we always had the luxury of time, and we enjoyed being frugal and inventive. Everything in our home has a story behind it and a connection to a place and the people we love. You see that our cozy home is a long-time gifting of family, friends, and neighbors."

Dianne and Paul lived in Ann Arbor, Michigan, before coming east. Paul was a biologist, and neither of them had ever built a thing in their lives. A brother-in-law in New Hampshire sent them a Boston Globe article about the Shelter Institute, which offered three-week classes on inexpensive home construction. The Schelbles dropped everything, sold their house, moved east, and joined a course.

A tiny twelve-by-eighteen-foot shed served as their "camp-out" home while the family built their new one in Maine.

Their porch is an observation deck from which to witness the parade of seasons. It offers a wide-angle screen of weather and wildlife, quiet snowfalls, blanketing fog, spring rains.

All summer long, Dianne and Paul live out on the porch, whose large windows keep the weather at bay. The porch's high elevation seems to protect them from biting insects, making screens unnecessary. In summer, all indoor plants are moved out to the porch's edge. When the kids were small, Dianne's wall of plants kept them from falling overboard.

When they lived in New Hampshire, a one-year-stay in 1977, Dianne and Paul used to scour the weekly farm bulletin for building materials. When an ad appeared offering these expansive statehouse windows for five dollars each, they jumped at the opportunity and purchased as many as they could handle. These windows, with their wonderful old thick panes, actually determined the design of their house. Now they are set so that the rural landscape and sunlight roll right into the house during daylight hours, flooding it with soft light.

Right: This bright kettle, a prized find from a nearby antique tool store, sits always ready to serve tea.

Right Page: The Danish Lange cookstove was Paul and Dianne's first symbolic gesture of their new lifestyle. They purchased it during their one-year stay in New Hampshire, before coming to Maine. The door to the porch was a leftover from one of Paul's construction projects. Paul was able to serendipitously match the horizontal mullions in the door's window with the big statehouse windows on either side.

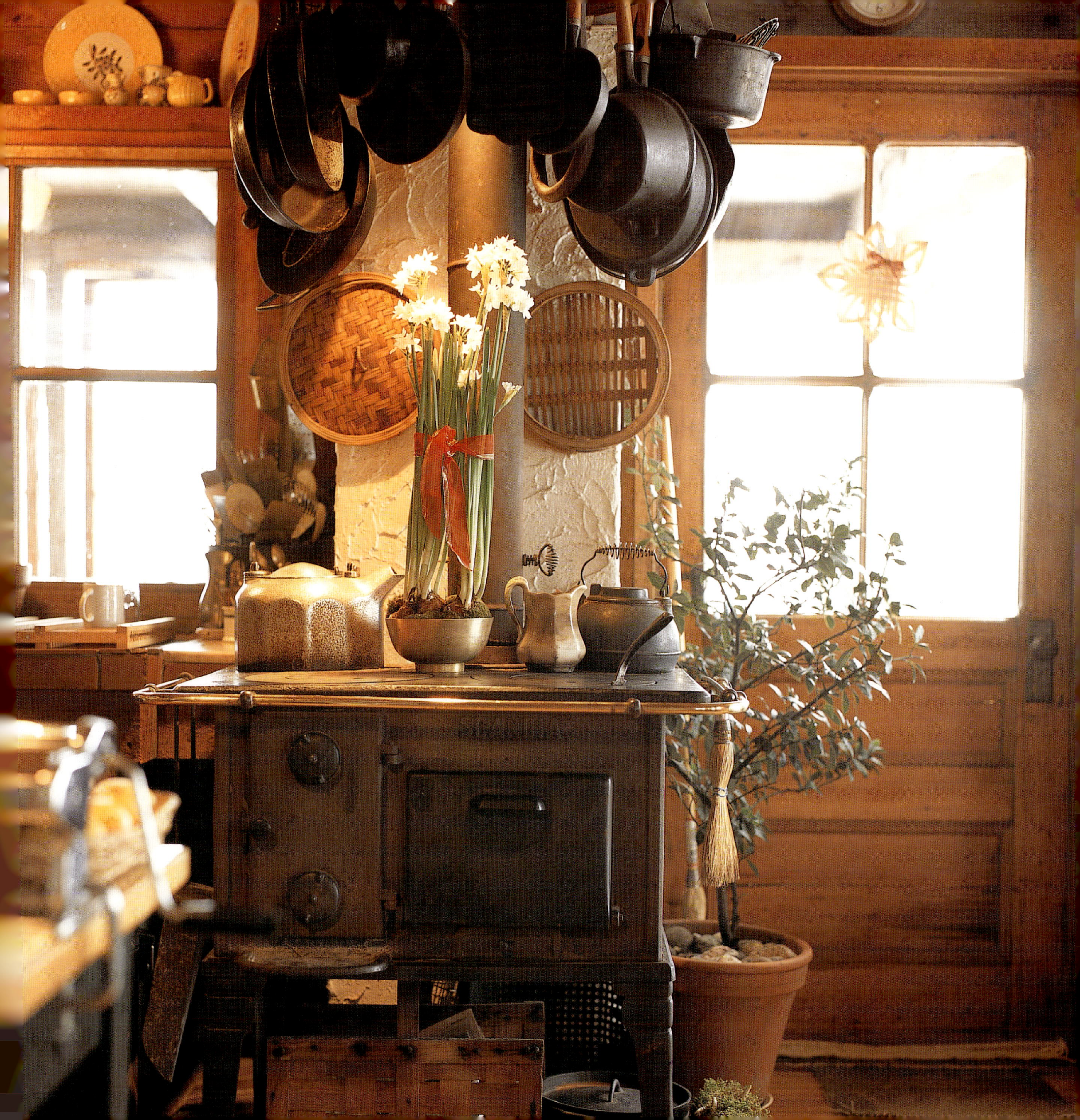
SCANDIA

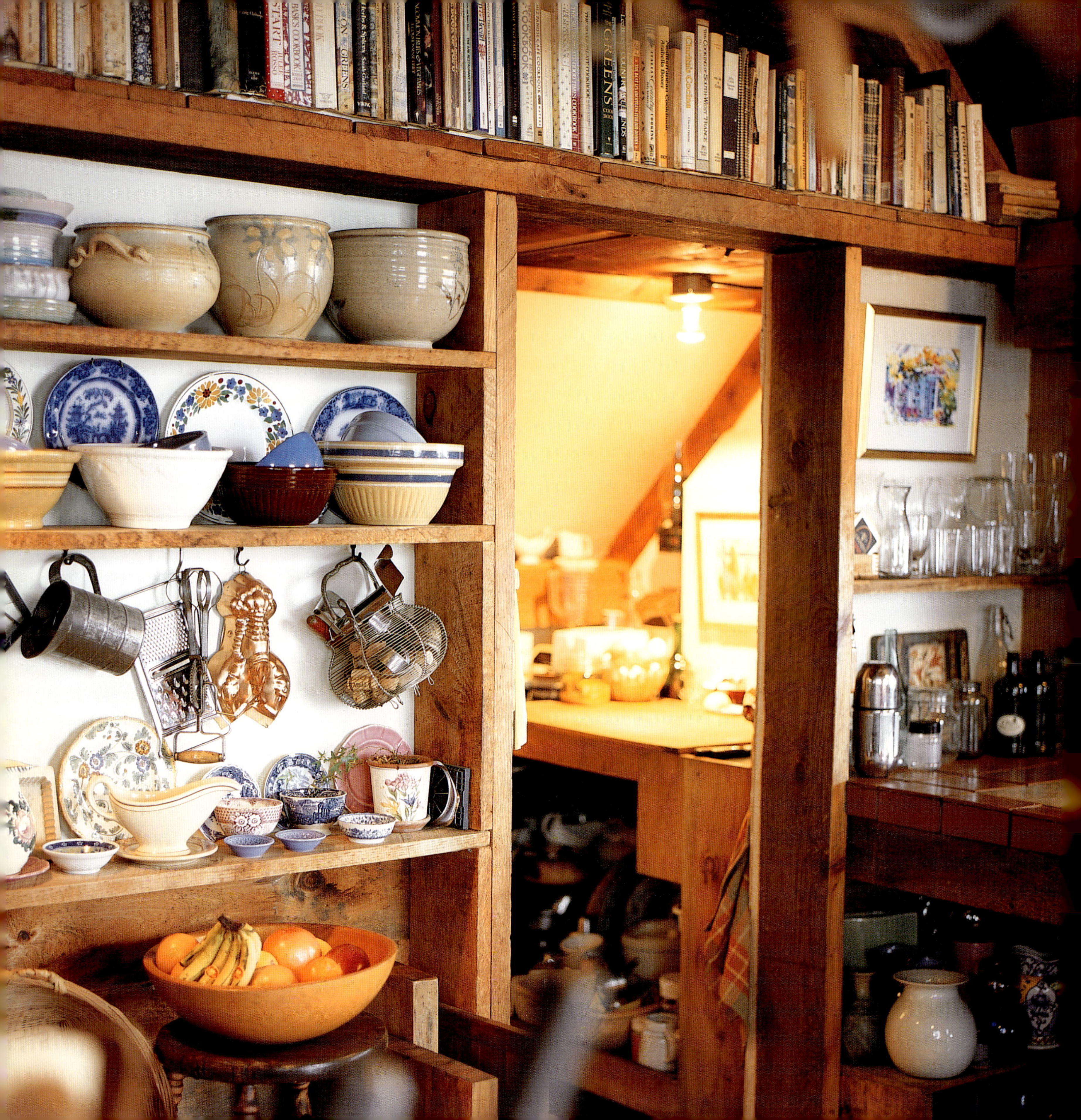

Left: A row of cookbooks and a composition of colorful china, pottery, and cooking tools supply charm and spirit to the room.

Below: One year the Schelble's ground their own wheat for bread-making. The Corona grinder, still available in Lehman's Catalog, a non-electric resource for home items, is mounted on the kitchen worktable. The tabletop is a piece of a bowling lane from the University of Michigan's athletic building that Dianne absconded with when the building was demolished in the early 1970s.

Above: Benches pulled to the dining table mean there's always room for one more. Generous views of the snowy fields spread out from the arched window.

Right Page: A room that truly reflects the people living in it is rare today. Many live in "resale" homes, with poorly built items purchased from catalogs of homogenized goods. Not so in this soulful nest. Paul's aunts purchased the cushy sofa in the 1920s. Over the years, Dianne reupholstered it along with the other stuffed chairs. The couch's purple velvet and bright ochre and moss pillows add a deep, mellow note to the atmosphere.

106 MAINE LIVING

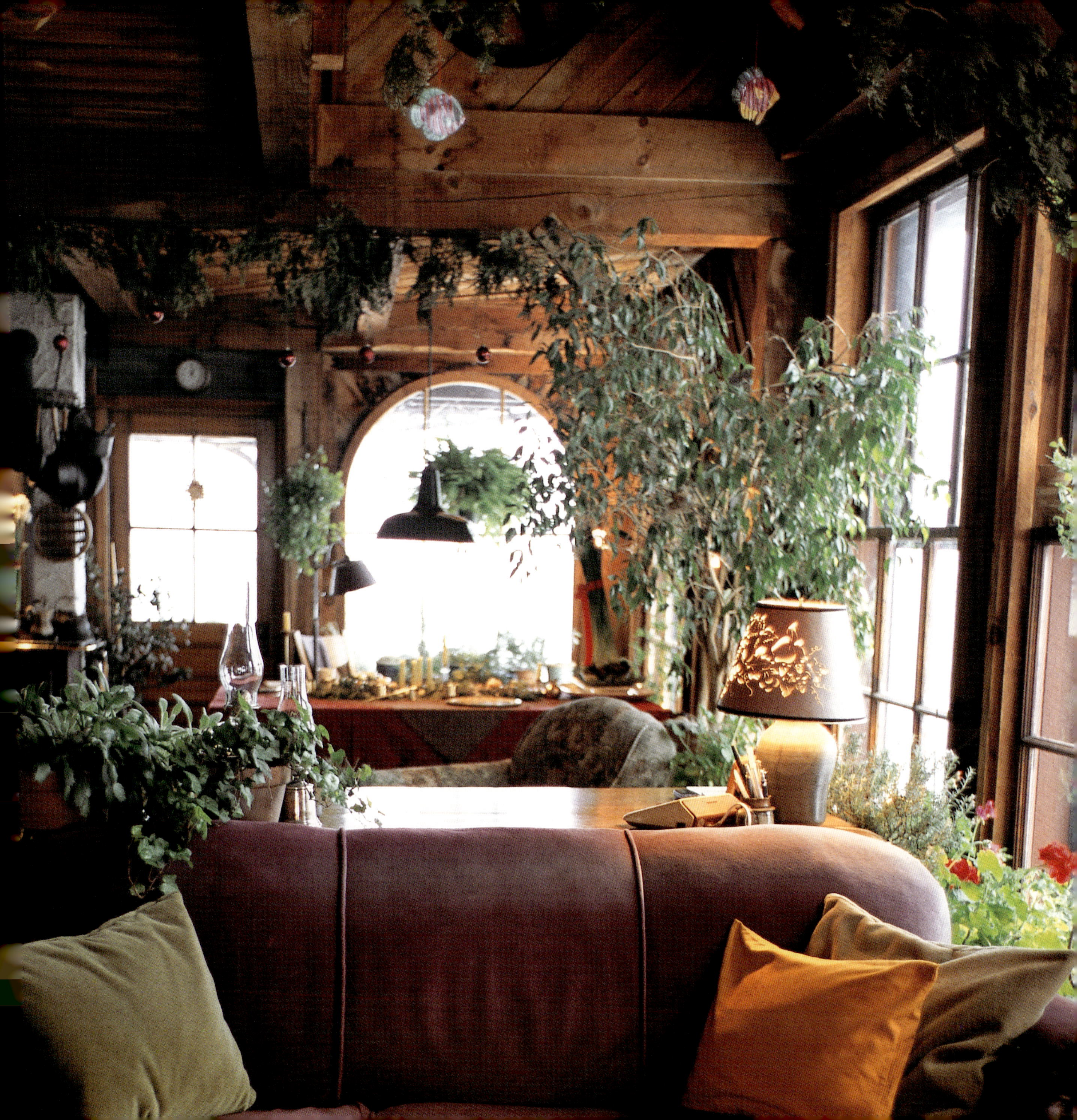

108 MAINE LIVING

BRING MAINE HOME

- Build your house around what you love, not what you think will improve resale value.

- Look for unique decorating items in unusual places, such as antique-tool shops.

- Keep cheerful geraniums blooming indoors during the frozen winter months.

- Line walls with beautiful crockery and interesting cookbooks.

- Recover a couch whose shape you love, in a deep, rich, wine color.

Left Page: A work of art, the woodstove in the living room is the house's primary heat source. A neighbor built it from scratch from a real boilerplate from the town's old blueberry-canning-factory boilers.

Above: Magenta and poppy-toned geraniums, safe from the snowy blizzard outside, bloom cheerfully near this bright window.

RURAL LANDSCAPES 109

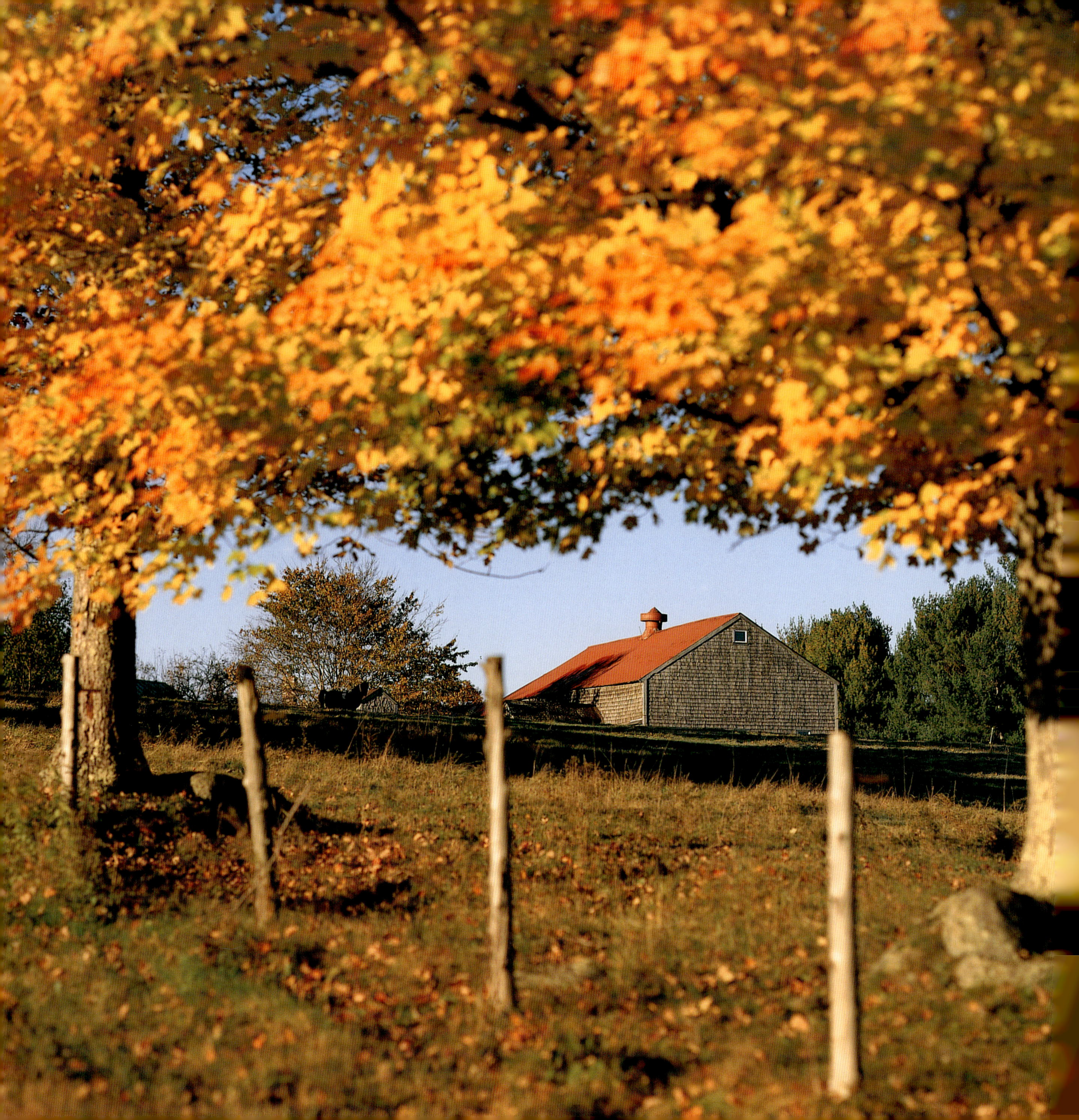

Rural Landscapes

Blueberry Hill Farm Bed and Breakfast

JoAnn Tribby and Ellis Percy epitomize the Maine lifestyle when they say, "Our lives are simple, pretty basic. We don't like a lot of frills. Less adornment means little interference with the important things. Beautiful hand tools, well worn and well maintained; vegetables gardens; healthy, loved work horses—these things bring us peace of mind and joy."

JoAnn's favorite times are spent outside caring for the animals. And mending the fences, that's a constant, she says. "We have lovely woods out back, where we walk all the time, on snowshoes and skis, and we do a lot of camping. Back awhile, there was quite a large family of beavers in the pond way back in the woods. We built a blind so we could observe their antics summer and winter. Unfortunately, a trapper killed them all one winter.

"I take the dogs for a run every morning through the blueberry fields," says JoAnn. She remembers the summer her son was two. "We walked right into a swarm of honeybees. It was surreal. I carried him all the long way home, with the bees following us. He was stung around fifty times, and I had more than two hundred stings."

JoAnn and Ellis's Scottish Highland cattle love to go for walks too, especially in the winter and when the snow gets high enough for them to scoot over the fence. "I used to fret and worry about them, but they always end up in the driveway at feeding time," JoAnn laughs.

Even such mundane tasks as laundry take on a meaningful simplicity at Blueberry Hill Farm. JoAnn even looks forward to it. "I love hanging the wash outside. It's my alone time. I double the lines all summer, but when it's really cold, our upstairs hideaway becomes a real Chinese laundry."

Jefferson is about fourteen miles inland from the tiny twin villages of Damariscotta and Newcastle. These towns are filled with beautiful homes and inns of the colonial period and sit at the head of the Damariscotta River, which runs twelve miles out to the ocean.

The road to Blueberry Hill Farm, known by many as the prettiest road in Maine, curls around farms and lakes and offers views over to the Camden Hills. JoAnn Tribby and Ellis Percy are surrounded by 125 acres of woods, hay fields, and blueberry barrens.

The farm, built in 1774 by Jonathon Noyes from Rowley Massachusetts, was passed down to the fourth son, Nathaniel, who fought in the Revolutionary War. He passed it on to his son, Abram, who passed it on to his son, Albert (all buried in the cemetery on the property across the lane).

In 1878, John and Mary Madden acquired the property and it remained in the Madden family until 1972, when JoAnn discovered it for sale one day.

JoAnn and Ellis operate their snug bed-and-breakfast year-round, hosting small summer weddings, anniversary parties, even holiday gatherings. For a fiftieth birthday affair one February, the menu featured homemade moosemeat stew and fresh, carrot birthday cake.

RURAL LANDSCAPES 113

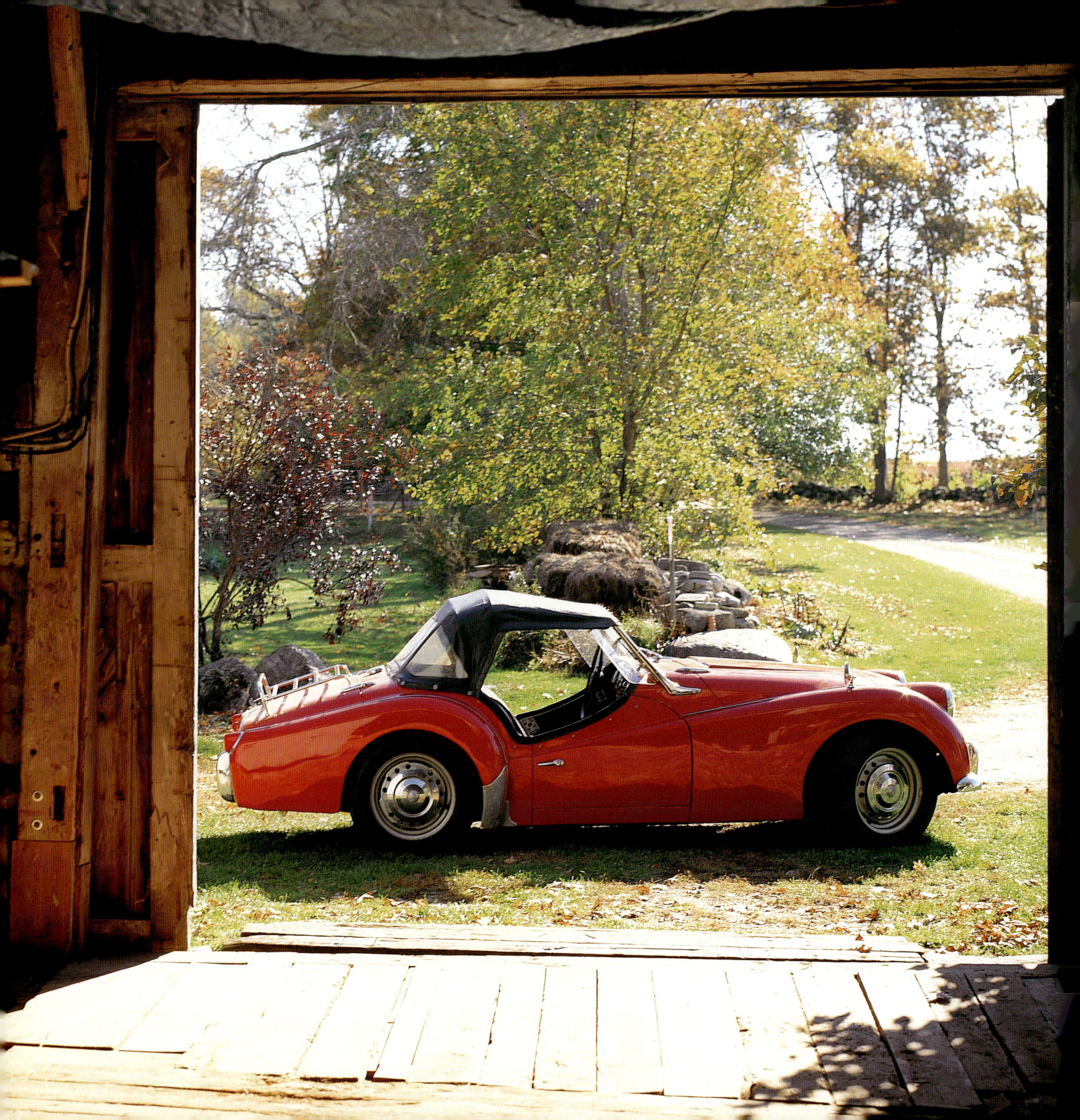

Above: The farm is certified organic and provides the eggs and sausage, peaches, apples, and many of the other fruits and vegetables that contribute to the morning's ample breakfasts.

Right: Ellis, a past president of the Maine Organic Farmers Association, owns Spruce Bush Farm across the lane. Ellis and son Rufus produce dilly beans, pickled fiddleheads and garlic, and each spring, a fresh batch of maple syrup. "Beyond Coffee," their newest product, made with organic herbs and spices, is sold through whole foods markets.

Left: The 1959, red TR3A, an everlasting project, stays around for weekend escapades.

RURAL LANDSCAPES 115

Above: Wind and Wooly Antiques, JoAnn's former business, provided plentiful inventory for the B & B.

Left: Charles Lindenman, JoAnn's father, made these walking sticks during his visits to the farm. They stand ready for exploring the woods behind the house or the lanes through the blueberry barrens surrounding the farm. The antique blueberry rake hanging above the sticks is still used by these organic farmers for picking their own berries.

Right: The porch, with its merry gingerbread trim on the east end of the house, was added in the early 1900s, and was quite certainly influenced by cottages being built at the time on the nearby coast.

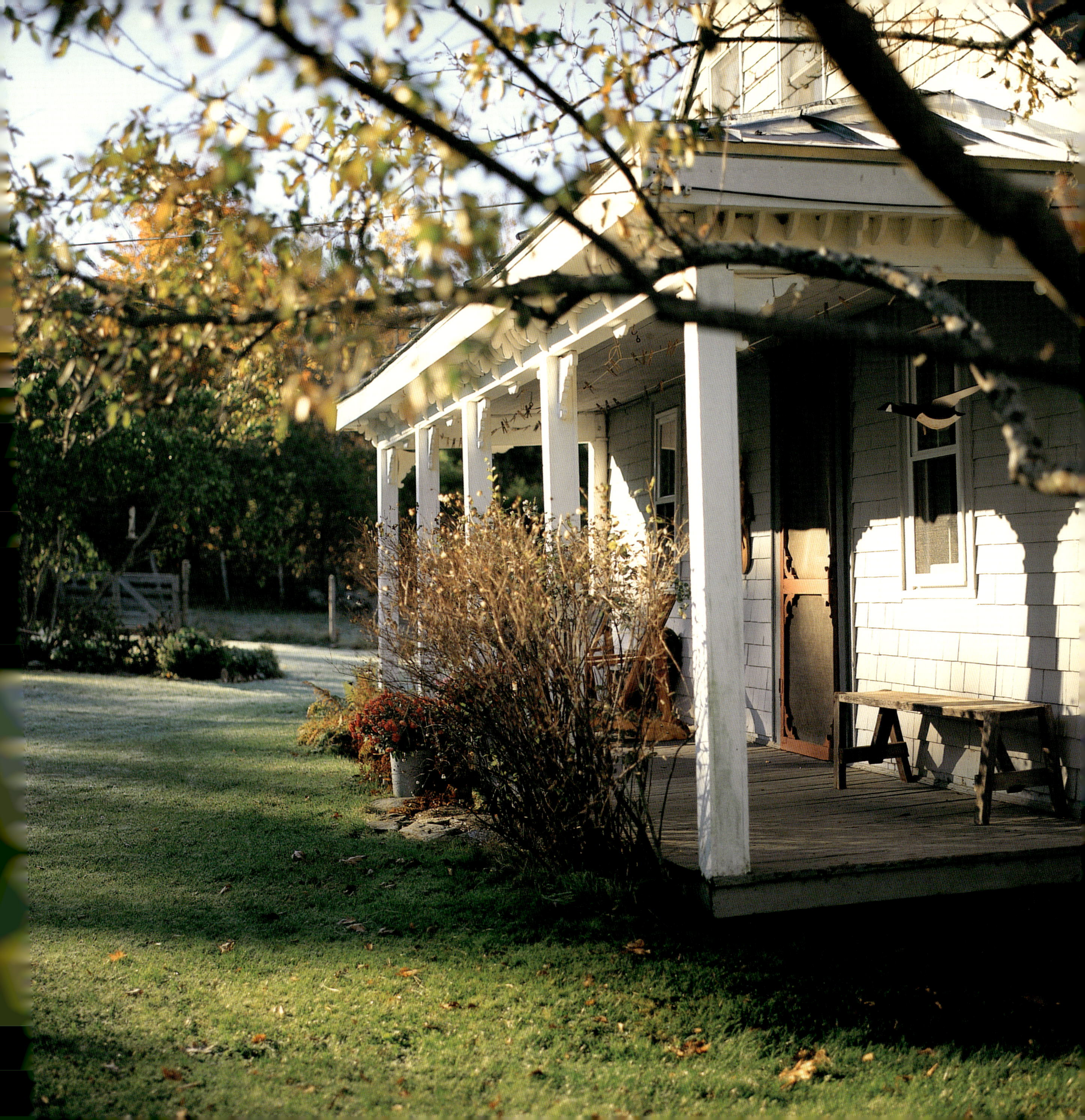

Left Page: A lighthearted horseshoe hung above the door guarantees good luck to those who enter.

Right Page: JoAnn loves the combination of apple-green and buttery yellow and uses it to brighten the space.

The fanciful tones spark the energy and pep up the myriad hues and textures of old, honeyed wood.

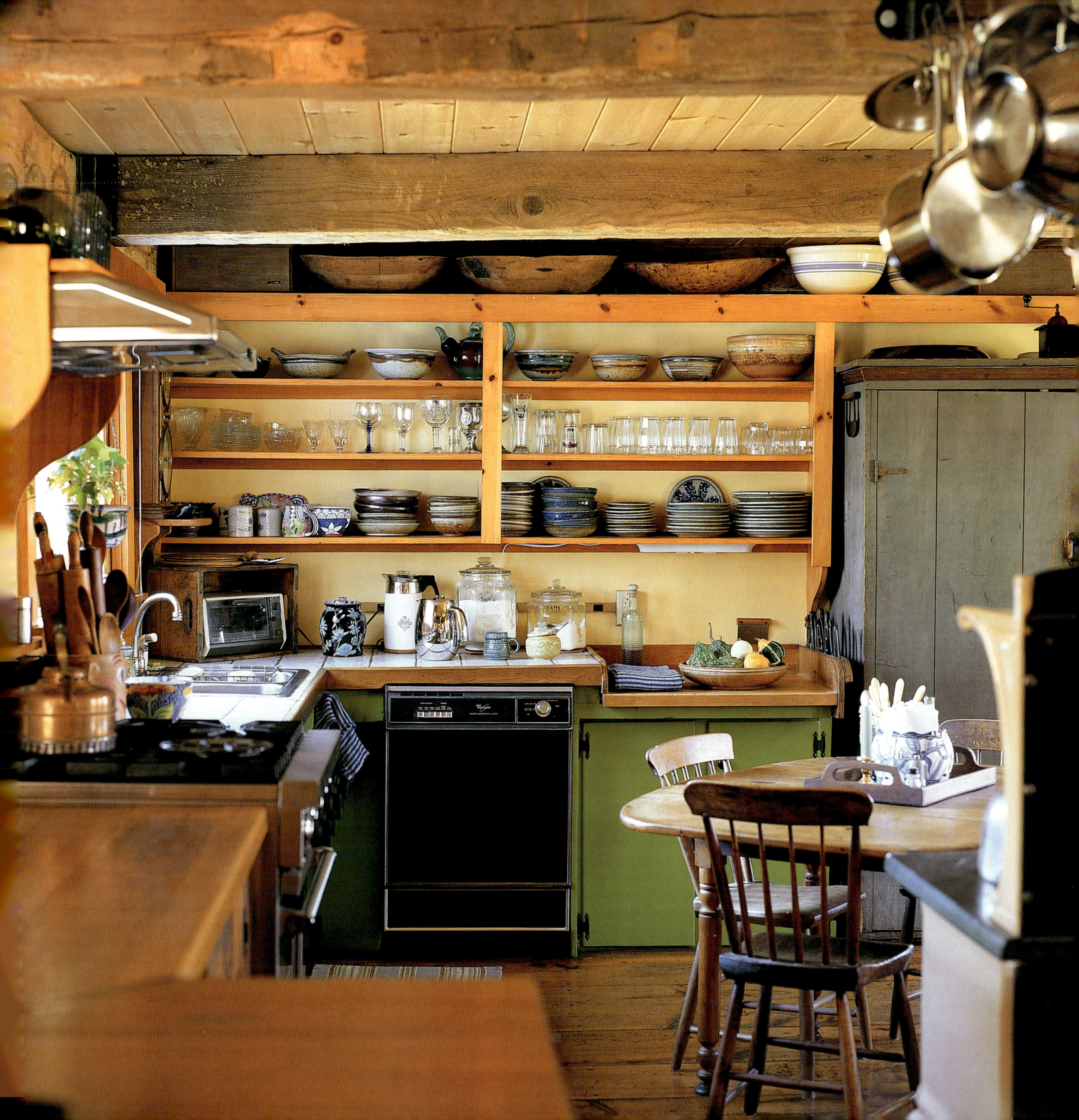

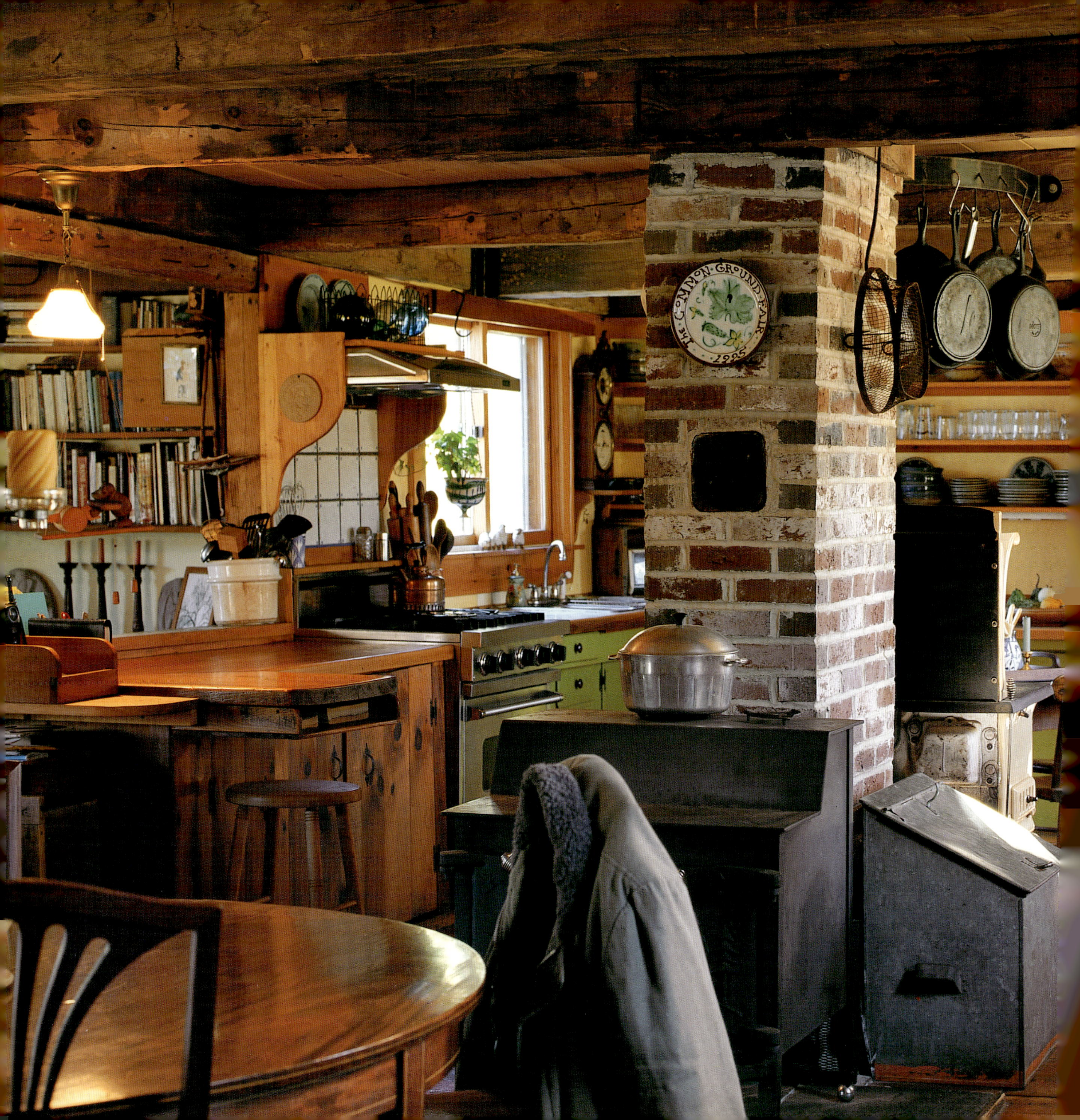
The COMMON GROUND FAIR
1995

Left: This kitchen and dining space were once part of the barn.

Being inside near the woodstove on a frosty morning feels like being covered with love. Ellis's favorite breakfast on a morning such as this is baked beans, sausage, and eggs.

Sons Rufus and Jon helped Ellis build the open kitchen shelving and put in a new ceiling that exposes the original log beams. Beautiful stoneware plates and bowls, made by a sister in California, are used every day.

The round dining table belonged to JoAnn's grandmother. Ellis made the hutch on the far wall that stores their dinnerware.

RURAL LANDSCAPES 121

Above: Historically, this east-facing bedroom was the parents' room. The rest of the family working the farm slept upstairs in the attic.

The bed, once owned by Connecticut Quakers, still has its horsehair mattress. The room's door opens up to the tiny vestibule in the front of the house.

Right: The Madden family diary from 1899 attests to the quiet, hardworking lives this farm housed. An entry each day expresses the moment at hand: "April 28th…shingled the back kitchen." "May 6th . . . Olive had a bull calf."

BRING MAINE HOME

- Hang wash out to dry on a line in your backyard.

- Mix and match colors and textures of wood; don't try to make your wood furnishings match.

- Display interesting pieces of family history; old journals, black-and-white photos, beautiful marriage certificates or marriage licenses.

- Brighten dark corners with a splash of buttery yellow paint.

- Renovate to expose your house's rich wood beams.

- Collect old wooden bowls and paint them with your own designs.

RURAL LANDSCAPES 123

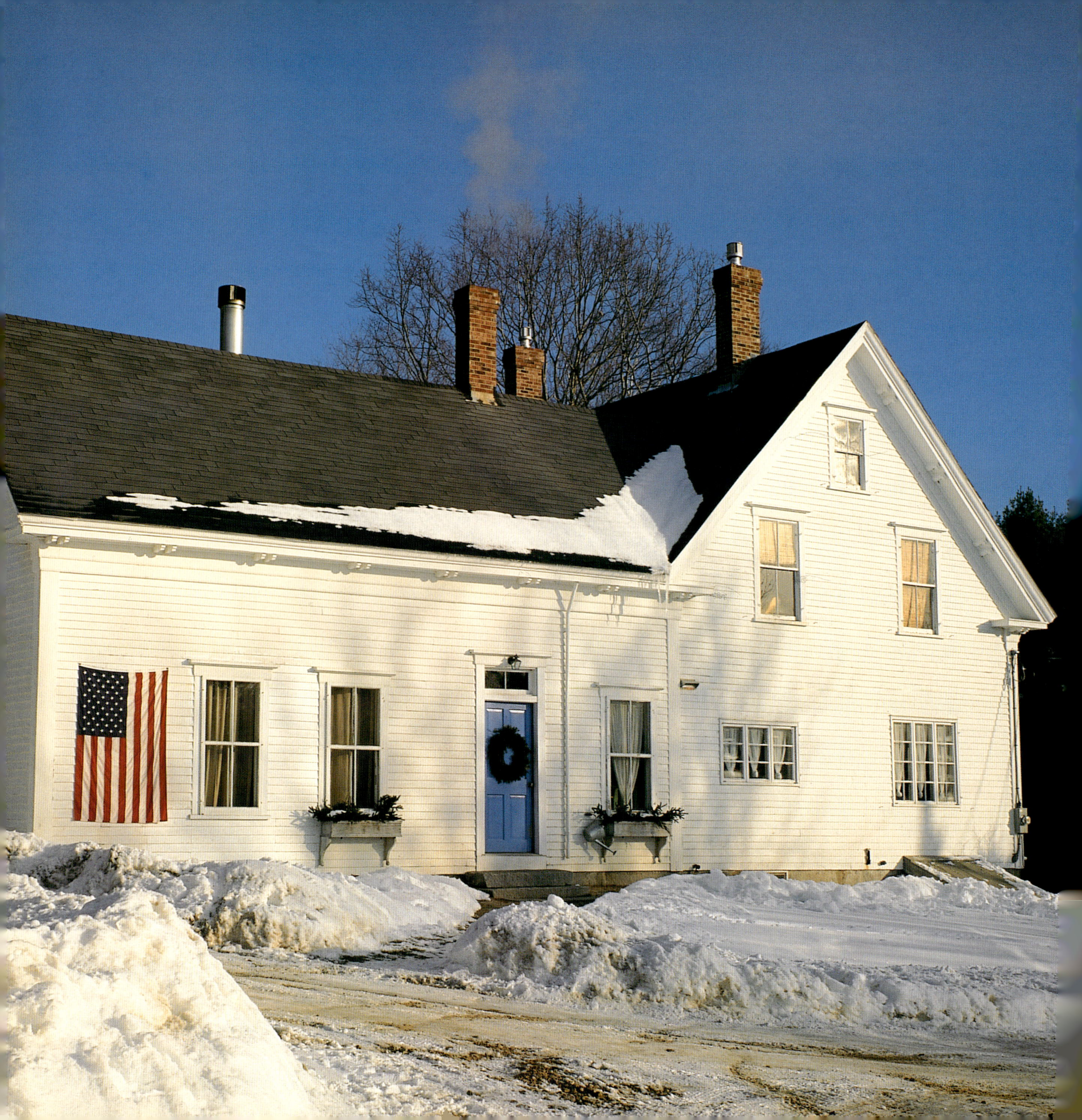

Rural Landscapes

Colorful Kennebec Farmhouse

Haley and Bill Eberhart never set out to define their tastes and preferences as purely "Maine." Yet as you walk around their home and grounds, you become very aware of the architectural history and tradition of the Maine coast and the Maine farm. "In some ways our home can be linked to the values of most Mainers: thrift, self-reliance, and individual responsibility, but with a willingness to stretch the rules and boundaries," says Bill. "There is no doubt that we love color. Our home is like a Van Gogh painting; it makes us feel good. Our home is also a reflection of our family. There is a great deal of love going on here."

Finding the farm was pure serendipity. "We drove past in June 2000, as we were headed north to look at another piece of property," Bill continues. "We turned around immediately when we saw its "For Sale" sign, cancelled our appointment, and arranged to see the farmhouse within the hour. We made our offer instantly."

"Billy and I run an old inn (the Grey Havens) on the coast and it was time for our family, who had shared two tiny loft bedrooms on the third floor, to spread out," Haley says. "We had been sharing our lives with the guests for twenty years and the time had come for us to have a place of our own."

Clementine, their youngest child, wished for a dog, and Haley says, "I was looking forward to playing with interiors. Guests at the inn, who have been returning for years, have lovely memories of their rooms there and any change to them had to be subtle. But I anticipated a house that allowed for a 'trial and error' approach to our ideas. I love our house's lime-green room"

Bill and Haley's classic Maine farmhouse, built in the 1890s, hugs a winding river road, "the prettiest in Maine," Haley says with her bright smile. A stately wall of evergreens on its northeast side shields it from the arctic winds.

The house stands tall on several acres of meadows. On midsummer nights when the Perseid meteor shower begins to host its phenomenal show, the Eberharts head to "the pit" in their field, where they start a roaring fire, lean back, and watch the heavens.

Right: The primitive green bench, from a Texas antiques shop, hints of a margarita flavor.

The Eberharts don't buy paintings; they create their own. Two startlingly bold ones—a bright pear and an apple—set the joyous and open tone for the way life is lived here. Painted by Bill, they were placed over the sink early one morning as a surprise birthday gift for Haley.

Left Page: Molly, their mellow Springer, who came to the family via a friend who could no longer keep her, welcomes us from her perch on the granite steps. From the outside, the house is classic Maine, all puritan and proper, but inside the atmosphere explodes with color-gone-wild in a spacious, clear, and bright atmosphere.

Left: For "kitchen junk" storage, a twenty-drawer chest in the kitchen corner closest to the dining room is home for all small important things. One drawer holds measuring spoons, one keeps the kids' snacks, another is the pasta drawer, and another holds all the cloth napkins. Everything is organized and at easy reach. This flea market bonanza, discovered by Billy, was another grand birthday gift for his Haley.

Right: "The Margarita Room," drenched in hot lime paint, cheers anyone nearby and spices up the whole house. A darker-toned trim and shelves make the space snap. Shallow hallway cabinets hold polka-dot glassware and serving pieces. The bold colors draw you through to the family hideout and den, where generous deco chairs settle around a welcoming hearth.

Above: One of Haley's passions is clicking through Web pages for "just the perfect finds." She enjoys it almost as much as scouring the aisles of local flea markets. The polka-dot deco coffee grinder was a prize Web discovery. (Haley's prowess at thrifting on the web was proven when a recent family wedding in Texas required that everyone wear purple dresses. She discovered seven purple dresses and pairs of shoes, in varying sizes and styles, on the Web; plenty to choose from for herself and her four daughters.)

RURAL LANDSCAPES

Left: A round table complements the square space, and works well for their large family. To make it, Bill found wide pine boards in the local classifieds and mounted them to the base of his grandmother's metal garden table, which he brought from Ohio. A little white paint added charm and sits well beside a built-in white china cabinet. Bill's home-made, one-of-a-kind table adds a touch of family history and loads of heart. The family's favorite colorful majolica gives it spice.

Right Page: Walls of cerulean blue anchor the dining room, giving it a powerful—almost ceremonial—charisma. The color calms, but invites curiosity. The color's dominance works well because the space is clear and uncluttered.

The Eberharts see thriftiness as a challenging game and an opportunity for creativity. Their resourceful attitudes always lead to surprising solutions.

130 MAINE LIVING

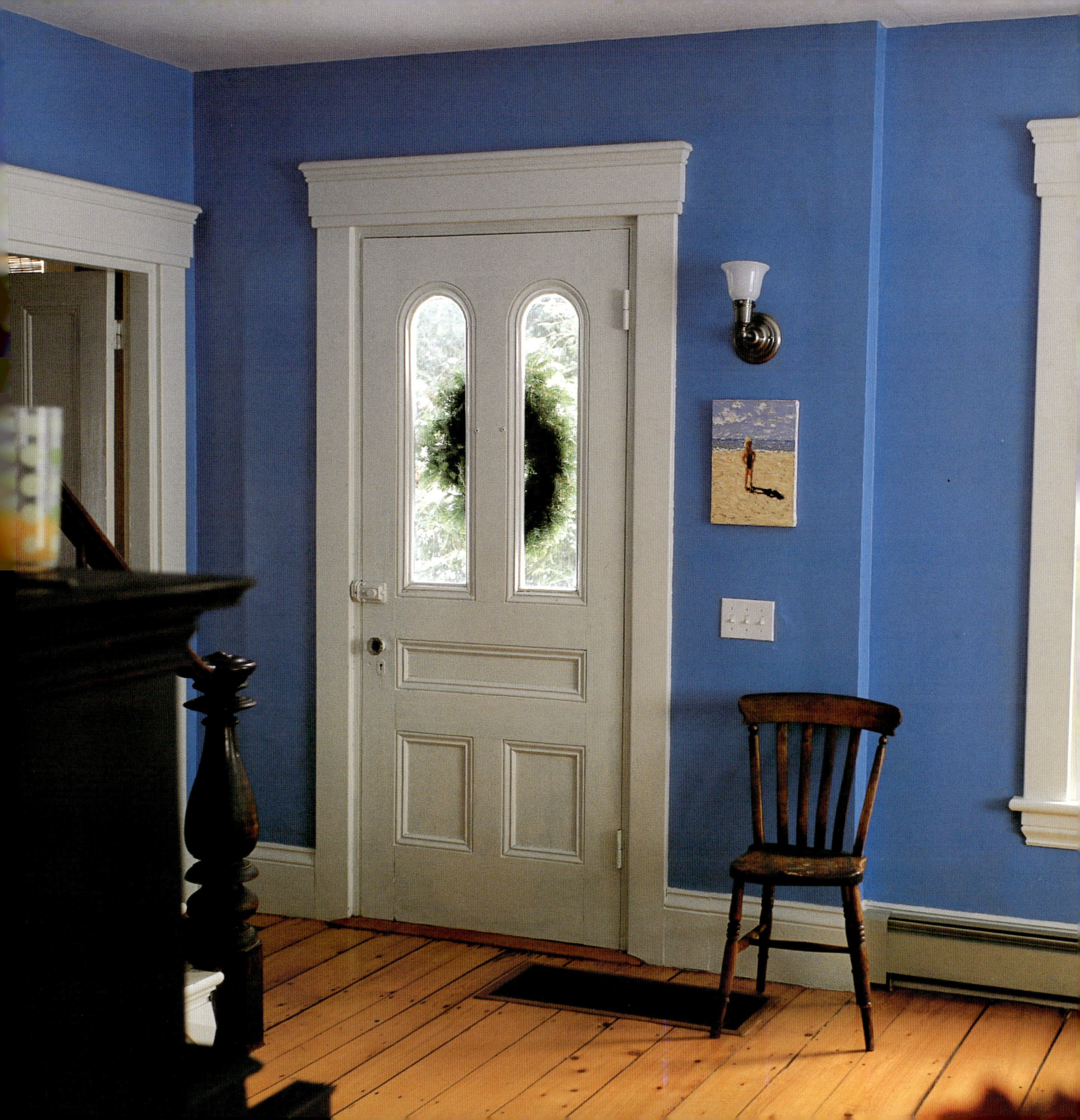

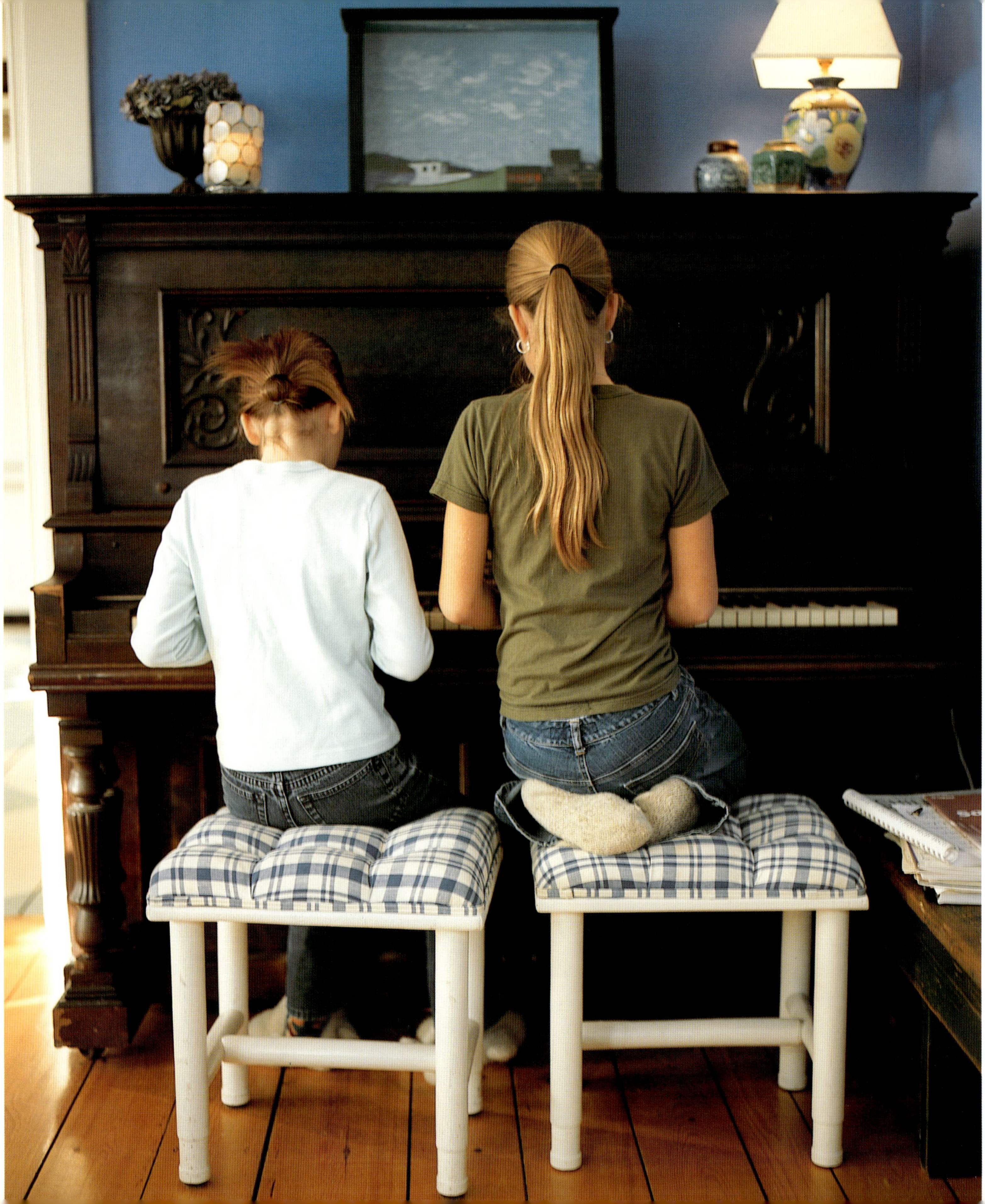

Left Page, Above: Clementine and Cady, excited about the holidays, move easily from piano duets to making felt stockings and ornaments, to their entrepreneurial project: creating old-time pot holders they sell at their family's inn, the Grey Havens.

Bill's compelling shadow boxes (one is atop the piano) are set throughout the house. He constructs these small theaters of Maine coastal scenes out of old wood and fishing-boat models, then paints in a world of water and sky.

Above, Left: Clementine's tropical watermelon room is a hot place to be on this winter day. Her budding collection of rubber duckies makes faithful and happy company.

Each child chose his/her own wall color and painted his/her own room.

134 MAINE LIVING

Left: Mary Kate's soothing space is filled with the old-fashioned charm and grace of a hug from her Texan grandmother. The breezy mixture of flowered curtains and plaid blanket feels like a Texas bunkhouse; their pale shades and gentle forms make a winning composition. The hot-pink pillow smacks like a hot kiss on a cool night, while the Van Gogh prints reflect similar qualities of her own room and her view from the window of the Maine landscape.

BRING MAINE HOME

- Give something in your house a bright new color—beet, green-apple, sunflower, mango. Even one old chair in a new color can add excitement and raise your spirits.

- Paint your kitchen floor in a diamond pattern.

- Create an inviting entrance to your home by painting your front door a bold color.

- Paint your own art, frame it, and display it.

- Make old-fashioned potholders with the kids for them to sell or use as gifts.

RURAL LANDSCAPES 135

Rural Landscapes

An Architect's House in the Snow

For architect John Silverio, Maine isn't just home: it's the only place home could be. "I don't think that I could have ever done the work that I have if I lived anywhere else. I'm really alive in this northern coastal region. The natural elements are so strong and active here. The landscape cries out for shingled, handmade, wood-heated houses. They look right in the fog, or with snow on the roof, or just sparkling in the sun. They look right connected to sheds and out-buildings by narrow footpaths through the woods, multi-faceted and tiered like spruce trees. My buildings feel at home with the shingle houses, grange halls, and boat sheds that were here before. I like to see houses interspersed with vegetable and flower gardens, to see animals on the land and things like wood piles and stone walls."

Right Page: Only after the house and John's architectural studio were completed did Susan and John construct the barn, an endeavor that took most Saturday afternoons over a two-year stretch to complete. A neighbor's brother shingled the roof and the Silverios' son Matthew later contributed the cupola.

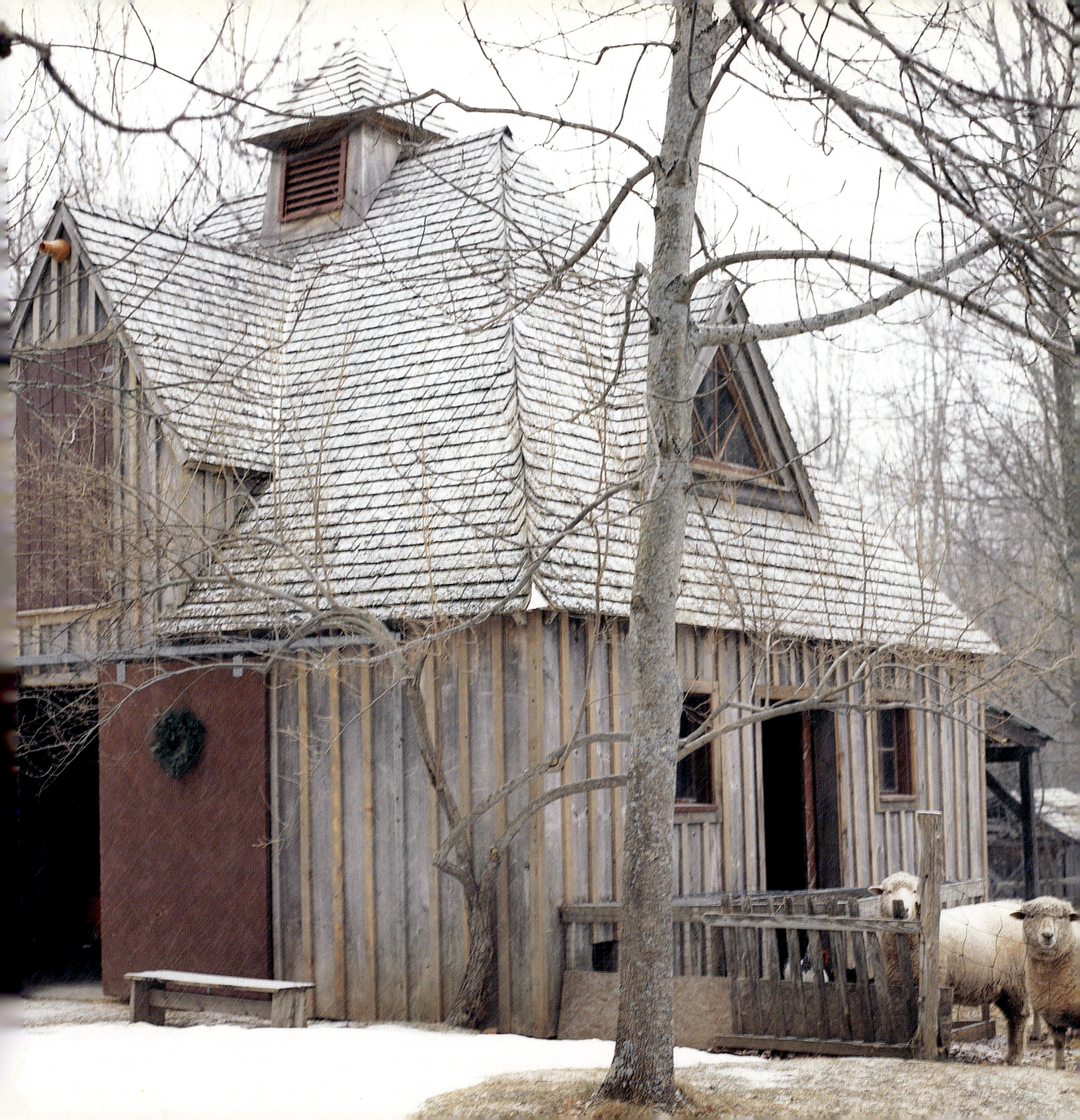

Left: A little red school, once a tiny cabin brought in by the Silverios to serve as a guest bedroom, sits in a stand of birch and ash trees now housing the Ashwood Waldorf School.

The school began here with Susan as its first teacher. The folktale-like structure has experienced three evolutions accommodating a growing enrollment. Presently, Susan and a colleague have a class of fourteen children between ages three and six. Inside, it is as cozy and protective as a hobbit house, with a rounded open space for the main room. Curved archways invite entry to the "quiet room," the kitchen, and bath.

The schoolchildren frequently walk by John's studio. One parent reported to Susan that her children have a new game at home called "architect," where they walk around the house with a roll of paper under their arms and point to things.

Right: John says of his houses, "They look right in the fog, or with snow on the roof, or just sparkling in the sun."

Susan explains how Maine became home for the couple. "Moving to Maine was a blind urge, like salmon swimming upstream. Our land was part of an old farm, a mixture of pasture and woodland in a small-town setting near the coast. All of the old farm buildings had completely tumbled down, but the land was high and well drained, at the end of a long dirt road, and we spotted a good house site that even had a hand-dug well close by. Since the last of the leaves have dropped, the wells have been filled with water again."

Both John and Susan appreciate Maine's seasons, but, as Susan says, "Winter is a most inward time of year—the gardens are long put to bed, the wood stacked, and the fires kindled regularly. The trees creak in the cold winds. All life forces have retreated to deep within the earth."

In Knox County, several miles inland from the mid-coastal villages of Northport, Camden, and Lincolnville, John and Susan Silverio have carved out a world for themselves in the middle of the woods. Once a bustling colonial farmland community, the rolling hills once again offer opportunities for a tranquil and rustic life.

Each of these structures seem to have grown slowly out of the land over the years, like tiny spots of lichen slowing expanding outward.

Very small—only 1,000 square feet—the house comprises three stories. They stand stacked like cubes one on top of the other, each layer smaller and rotated, as if a child, lost in play, had stacked a pile of blocks. The roof, faceted like a crystal, is heedless to the weather. From a distance, the overall appearance seems rather like a large pinecone dropped in a clearing of the woods.

John's work has long been influenced by Norwegian stave churches and Russian log churches. "They have qualities that I admire, such as ascending forms, emerging and unfolding shapes, graduated proportions, and a feeling of radiance."

The parking is left closer to the dirt road, and the narrow, woodsy approach to the house is a flowing extension of the long dirt road.

Above: The barn framing was derived from a method found in an old USDA bulletin. Over this frame, vertical boards and battens were nailed.

Metal stakes hammered in the ground keep the barn doors from blowing and banging in winter blizzards and summer storms. The little red hen, retired from the egg business, is free to roam. She's the last one left of a flock that was visited by a fox one cold winter night. At times, she even allows the children to take her for short sledding trips. The Silverios' other hens are an Asian variety, most of them gentle creatures and very good layers. They supply John and Susan with just enough eggs for cooking plus, from time to time, a few left for sharing.

Right: Sheep require little care and meager shelter and were ideal for keeping the land cleared in the beginning. Years ago Susan learned to spin wool with other women in the midcoast area, and the sheep provided her with wool. She still enjoys knitting, although she now chooses her wool from other sources around Maine. Mother sheep Nilla and her twins Roly-Poly and Holy Moley now supply the kindergarten each spring with three bags full of their wool for doll stuffing and felting projects.

Right: Inside the house the tidy space feels like the belowdecks of a well-maintained boat—just enough room for everything. The cheery atmosphere brings to the surface those childlike qualities that we should never discard: caring, a sense of wonder, serendipity, openness, nonjudgment, trust. The red chairs and warm table invite good company and good conversation.

John designed the square extension table, and furniture-maker and friend Wayne Breda constructed the table with a curly maple top and cherry legs. Sitting close to the window, the table echoes the smaller square-within-the-square frames of the window, a familiar motif that inspires all of John's work.

Susan brings out the small, hand-carved angel for the holidays. It is a treasured heirloom from her grandmother Helen's house in Dayton, Ohio. She remembers noticing it on the table by her chair each time she would visit for Sunday dinner.

RURAL LANDSCAPES 141

Left: After years of keeping their pine walls and floors unpainted, the Silverios chose a creamy yellow shade for the walls and silver green for the floors. The colors give the room a warm, plantlike palette and brighten the space. The silver-green tone is frequently used on wooden boat decks.

Right Page: Pots of lavender and peace lilies sit on the stair landing along with an angel that Susan says "watches over our house."

A traditional stair railing would not work in this space of creative design solutions, and after about five years of being puzzled, the ingenious idea of a single, continuous railing, like a giant metal eyelash, finally came to light.

John's small watercolors, painted during an Irish retreat, follow the stairs up.

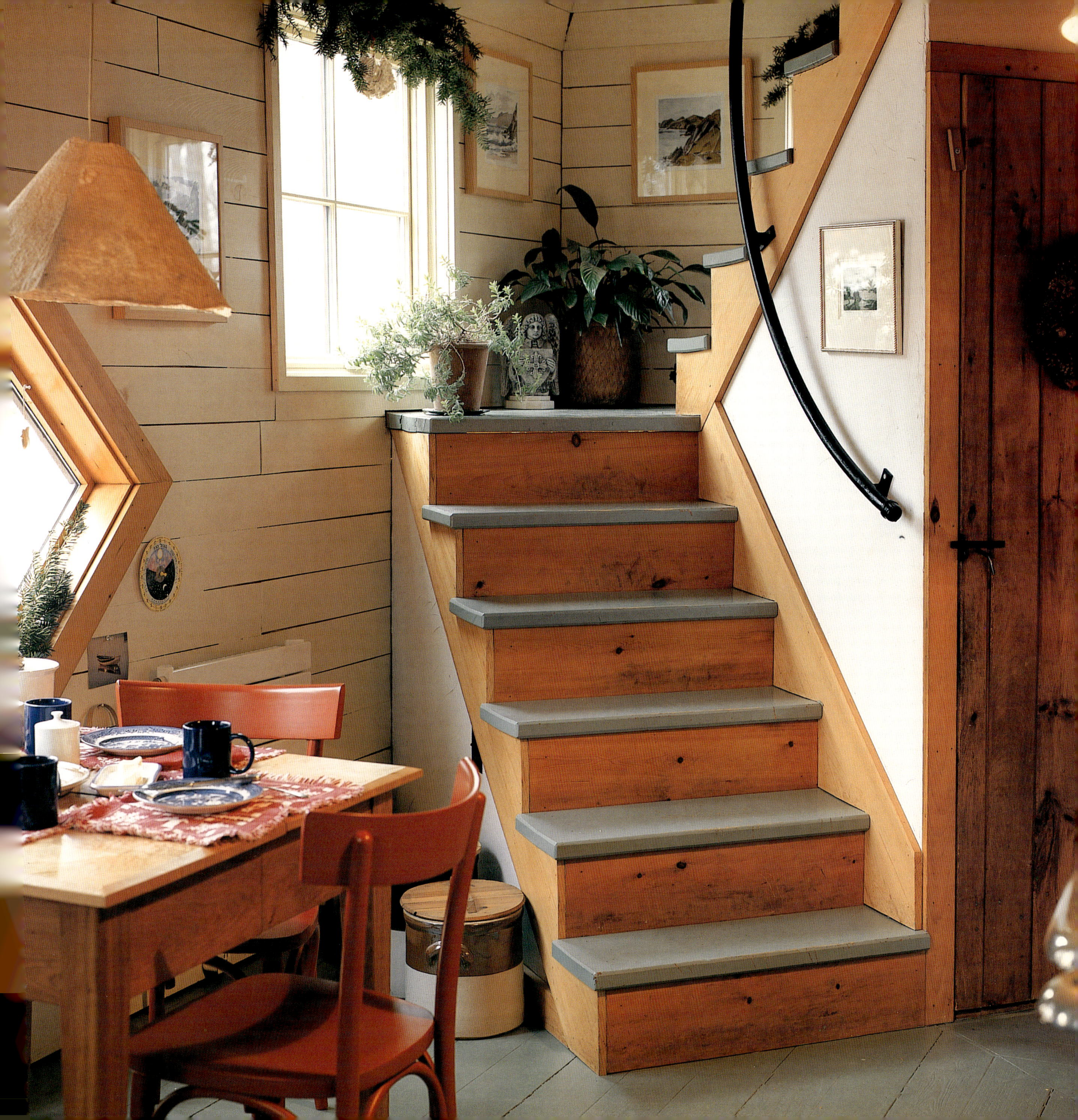

Above: Susan's knitting supplies rest in a Vietnamese rice basket, a Christmas gift from John. Wool socks, always needed and welcomed, are a very portable project. The new yarn is dyed to create a pattern when knitted.

Right: Warm flannel robes for cool Maine mornings hang on the closet door.

Right Page: The chapel-like ambience of the house is defined by the ceiling's log beams, radiating out from the heart of the house in a starlike design. The beams were cut from the wood on the property and hand-peeled by friend Sam Smith, who also did most of the house construction.

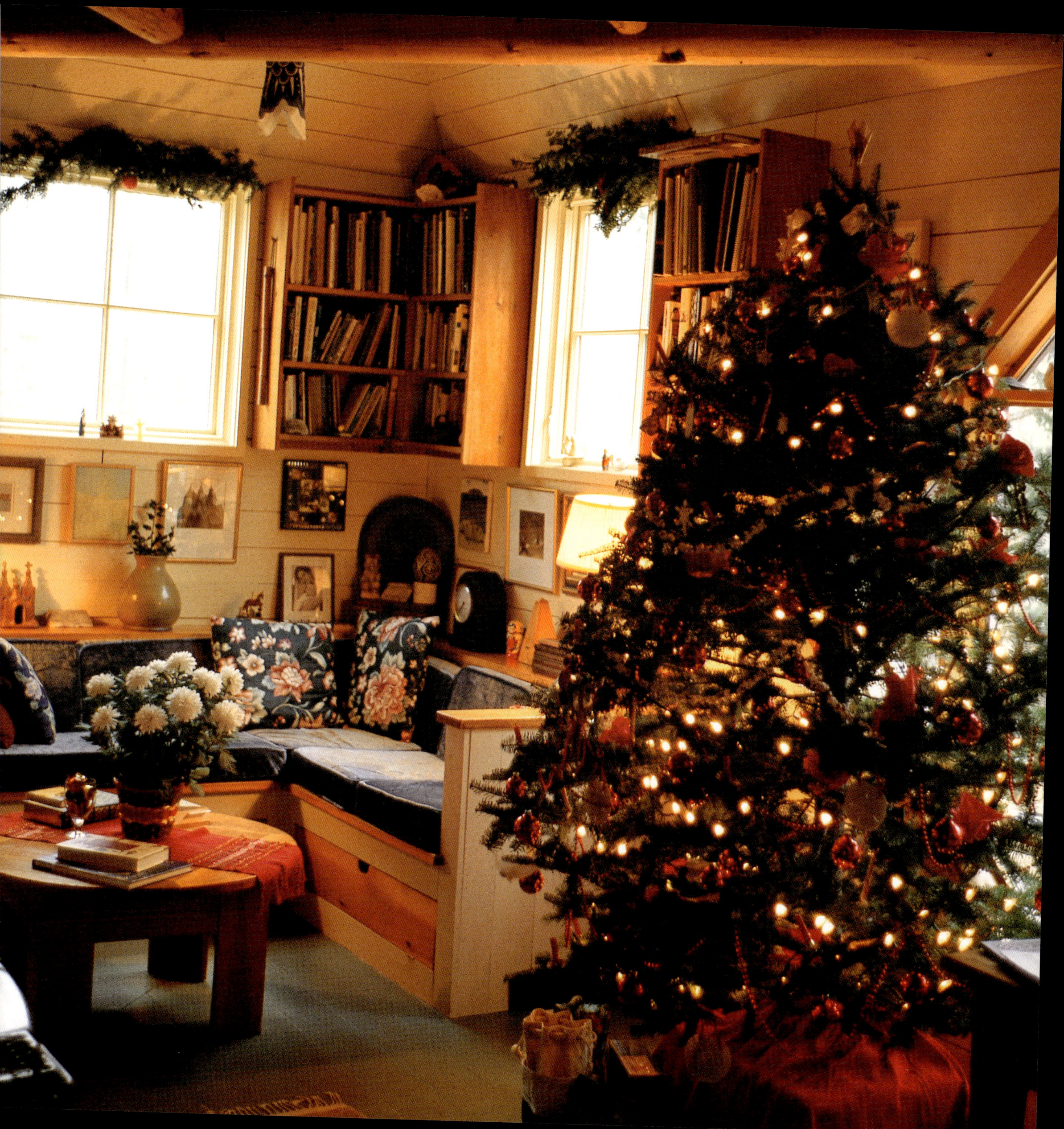

Above, Right Page: John's toys hang from the beams and perch all around his workspace. Seeing houses in simple, fresh shapes inspires him.

BRING MAINE HOME

- Use retrieved building materials such as used bricks and salvaged wood.

- Plant your own garlic; keep rosemary on the windowsill; grow a camellia in a sunny bathroom.

- Take the time to learn how to knit.

- Create flower and vegetable gardens, and write about them.

- Make blueberry pancakes or muffins from scratch, adding tiny sliced-apple pieces and walnut chips.

RURAL LANDSCAPES 147

Inland Lakes

Cobbosseecontee Lake Porches

The Abenaki Indians fished in Cobbosseecontee Lake long before the European settlers found their way to Maine. Also known as Cobbossee, Indian for "the water of many sturgeons," the nine-mile lake lies at the foot of the village of Manchester, halfway between Augusta and Wintrop. The lake drains southeast as Cobbosseecontee Stream flows into Pleasant Pond, eventually emptying into the mighty Kennebec River.

Back in the olden days Lake Cobbosseecontee was a retreat for Maine's political bigwigs. Cobbossee once had their own fleet of iceboats and held races each winter weekend. One of Maine's grand dames recalls that her family's ice-racing boat was named "Flirt," and as a child she was always terrified when they would leap in the air and fly over the open waters in the ice.

Priscilla Stevens not only adores her cottage but, unlike many homeowners, knows a good deal of its history. "The Gannet-Farnum Cottage was built in 1925 by William Howard Gannet, a well-known publisher from Augusta, Maine. It remained a summer retreat for over sixty years, until we discovered the property in 1987." At that point, they fell in deep, permanent love with the cottage. Against friends,' builders,' and engineers' advice, they decided not to tear it down and build anew. They treasured the cottage's unusual design and the fact that it was steeped in history. They wanted to honor it by bringing it back to life. "

"The original owners were really the early environmentalists," she adds. *"The original porch, only five feet from the water, had three tall white pines growing up through the roof."*

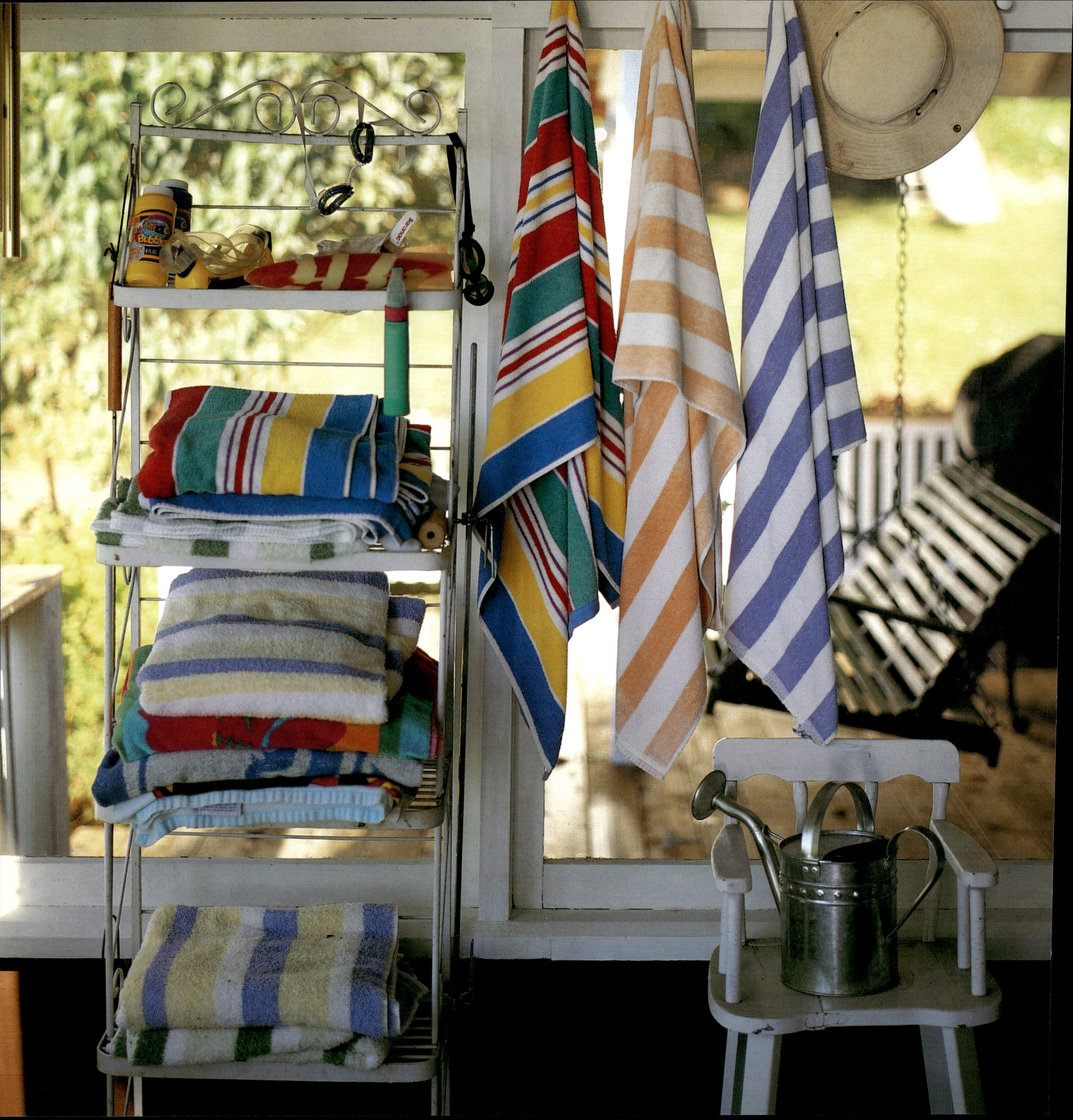

Right: "The white bunkhouse came with the cottage. It's turned into a retreat for our kids and their friends. We have cookouts in the fire pit nearby and make sticky s'mores. Everyone takes a turn telling ghost stories."

Left: Everyone has their own towel hanging in the corner, so they are "at least partially presentable for supper."

Inland Lakes

Red Cottage Porch

Kathy Cone says, "Our little red house was built in 1895 by a state legislator from Augusta and hasn't changed very much since then. We are hidden in the woods on the west side of the lake. Each summer's day is a gift."

152   Maine Living

Above: "We have every meal on the porch, and the 'seafood and pasta' sign is the family joke because that's what we seem to be cooking all the time!"

Above Right: "Mark is the furniture collector. He's found antiques for the whole house. I sometimes think the porch is too crowded with furniture, but when the family's here, there's never an empty seat."

Right: Mark and Kathy's collection of paddles seems to grow with their large flotilla.

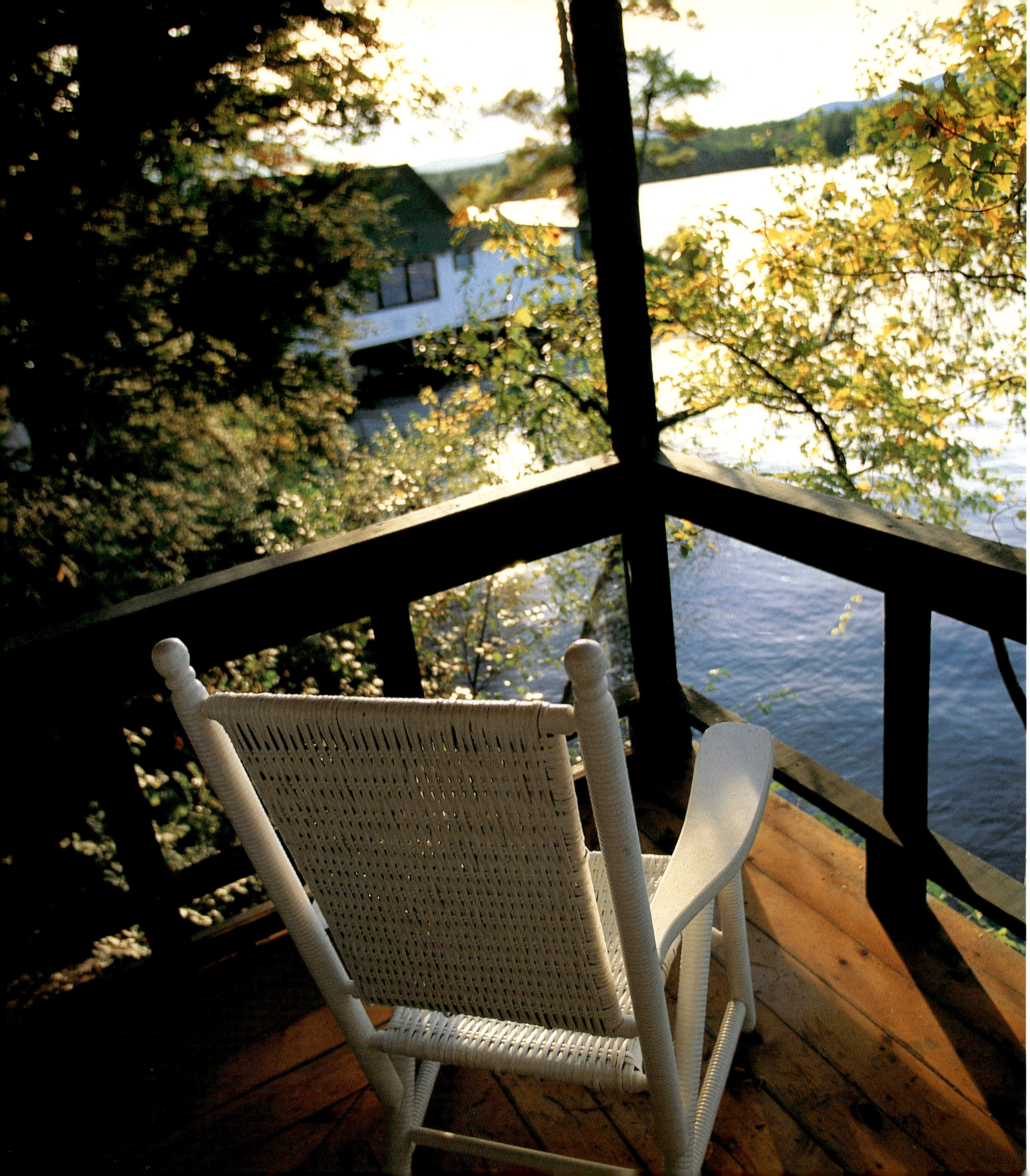

INLAND LAKES

Quisisana

Quisisana Resort, a summer camp that even most Mainers aren't aware of, on the shores of ten-mile-long Kezar Lake, was named for the Latin *quisisana*, "place where one comes to heal one's self." It embodies the combined healing powers of music, nature, and food.

Quisisana is a collection of camplike green-and-white "boxes" hiding among forty-seven heavenly acres of soaring pines gathered around a sandy-bottomed lake of sparkly, soft water.

The Presidential range behind the lake gives its own stunning performance, each evening featuring a glorious reflected sunset.

Guests, when they're not attending the evening's show, explore Maine's beauty by hiking, swimming, golfing, and antiquing. After an afternoon on the beach, *New York Times* crossword puzzle in hand, one may end up at the dining hall for samples of zucchini vichyssoise and salmon mousse, or pan-seared halibut with a passion-fruit-and-soy glaze.

An hour or two after dinner each evening, everyone gathers in the big music hall on the lake for the evening's performance. The resort's staff of aspiring musicians and actors, hailing from the nation's best music schools, such as Oberlin Conservatory, Julliard, and the New England Conservatory, present Mozart, Puccini, the *Music Man*, *La Bohème*, *The Marriage of Figaro*, and others.

Above Top: At the end of October, two months after Quisisana's season has ended, the piney woods are saturated with autumn's stillness and the cry of the loons that only the caretakers are there to enjoy.

Above Bottom: The landscape shows evidence of Maine's winterizing rituals. Pathway lamps that shone on summer nights are wrapped in black plastic, a protection from snow and ice. As we wander along the quiet pines, Larry, the resort's caretaker (who thirty years ago was a young performer and waiter himself) works with a crew to remove screens and board up doors and windows.

Above Top: Today the sun is warm enough for guests to swim in the lake's soft, silky water.

Above, Bottom: The mystical beauty of the setting combined with the green-and-white wooden-toy camps is Maine in its purest form.

Quisisana Hotel was built by Spenser and Madaline Strauss in 1917 as a summer retreat for musicians. In the early days, musicians came to the lake for camaraderie and the opportunity to play their music with each other out in the wild woods. By the 1960s, it was attracting such guests as Vladamir Horowitz, who thrilled everyone by hauling in his own piano and setting it up in his cabin.

BRING MAINE HOME

- Give a bargain wicker rocker a coat of fresh paint to brighten your porch.

- Let functional also be beautiful: let a simple metal porch shelf hold a tidy assortment of summer essentials: bright towels, sunscreen, goggles, a sunhat.

- Go swimming in a clear, cold lake in October.

- Rescreen your doors with copper screening.

- Treat yourself to salmon for breakfast regularly.

- Make balsam pillows for your loved ones by filling small cloth bags with fragrant balsam needles.

INLAND LAKES

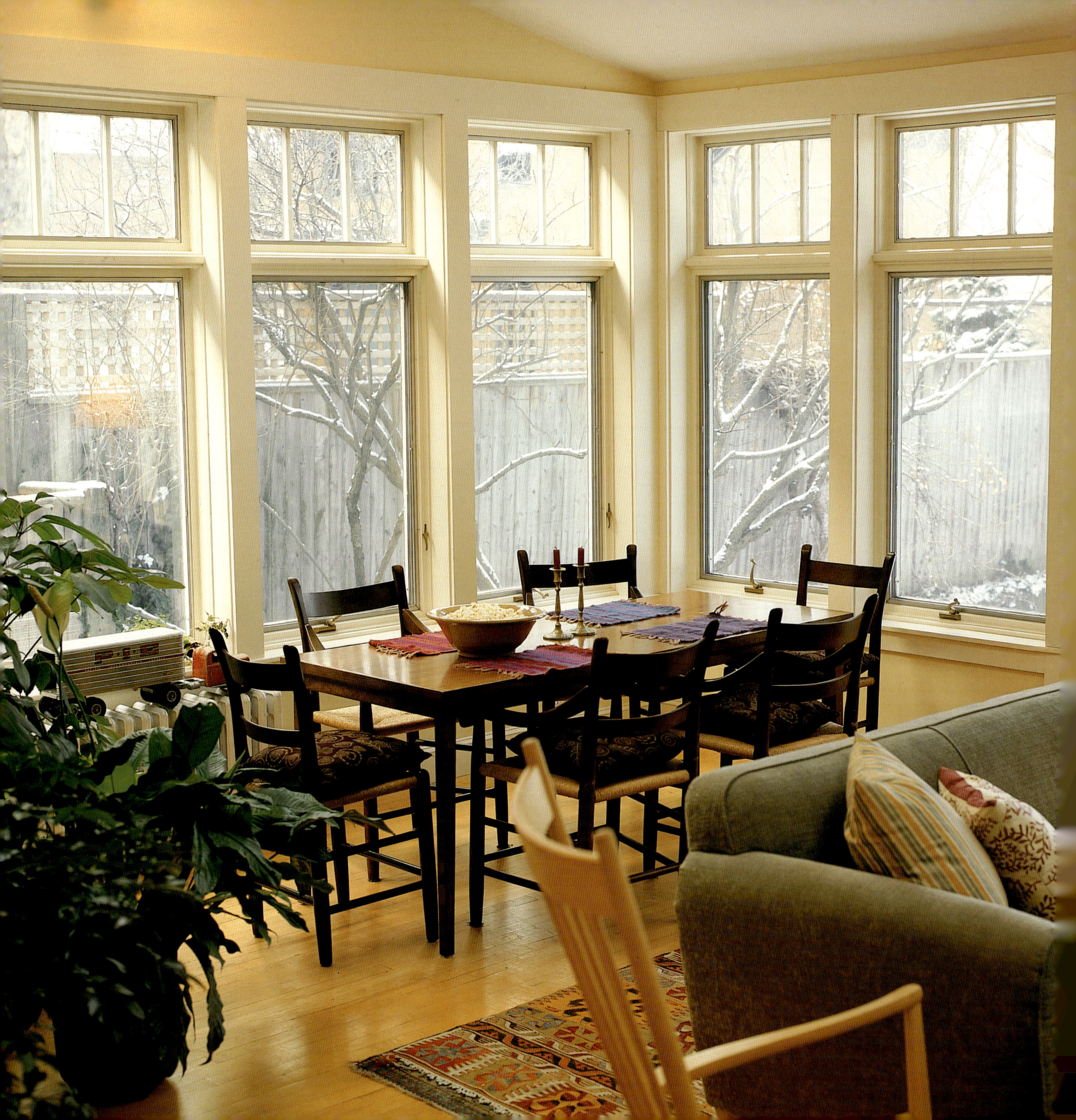

CITY DWELLING

Light and Space

Poet and novelist James Dickey is said to have defined a writer as someone who is enormously taken by things anyone else would walk by. Sam Van Dam thinks this applies to good architects as well. Details are certainly an inspiration for his own work. "Recently, as I walked out of the back door, I was astonished to see a scrap of lavender paper lying on the snow. Where did this color come from? When I brought it inside, it was just a piece of white copy paper, and so I learned something about the color of snow. Last fall, my wife found ladybugs on branches of a linden tree high above the street outside our third-floor window. Where did they come from? The colors of their backs are really quite wonderful. In Maine every year we can rediscover the change of seasons in infinite detail."

Left: The dining chairs with woven seats, were a spectacular deal. Sam had the dining table made from a solid-core door and stained it to match the chairs.

When asked about his own connection with Maine, Sam responds, "My father had a wonderful library of books on landscape painting—he had studied with Rockwell Kent and Will Barnet at the Art Students' League in New York. Images in these books of Monhegan and the Maine coast made quite an impression on me. Later, as a graduate student, my wife's mother let us use her cottage in Pemaquid for some long fall weekends. That was all it took.

"I came to Maine after a day at the Boston Public Library collecting names of all the architects I could find in about twenty telephone books," he explains. "I am interested in designing houses and additions that fully integrate the complexity of owners' needs and the specific qualities of a place and have the results seem inevitable. The architect William Wurster said, 'I like an unlabored thing, that looks as inevitable as something that comes out of a frying pan just right, like an omelet in France.'"

For Sam Van Dam, wife Jane Francisco, and their three children, Sam and twins Abigail and Peter, Portland is a beautiful place to live and work. The diversity of the population, the richness of the architecture, and the fact that it is a seaport make it a jewel of a city.

The birth of the Van Dam twins in 1984 was a momentous occasion that presented opportunities to rethink their living situation. Suddenly the old Georgian-Federalist home seemed a bit too intimate and too dark. The concept of light in an airy family space brought moments of peace and hope to the young parents. Sam was designing beautiful, light-filled, contemporary living spaces for his clients, so it was purely natural to have his work flow into his own home as well.

A glance from the living to dining room reveals a space as clear and articulate as Sam and Jane's manners and ideas. The atmosphere is direct and sophisticated; a very safe, erudite, and comforting harbor away from the workings of the office, deep in the heart of the city.

The three-light windows above the single-light casements are characteristic of the turn-of-the-century conservatories that Sam has noticed in their West-end neighborhood. The space soars and sings with the extra light.

Left: The woven magenta wool placemats are tokens from Sam and Jane's Greek-island honeymoon.

Right: The neighborhood is composed of gracious, stately brick houses. Portland's fire of 1866 devastated the city, so most homes were reconstructed with locally made brick. There is a wonderful orange to the clay, giving the houses rich, rusty tones. Bricks are still manufactured nearby.

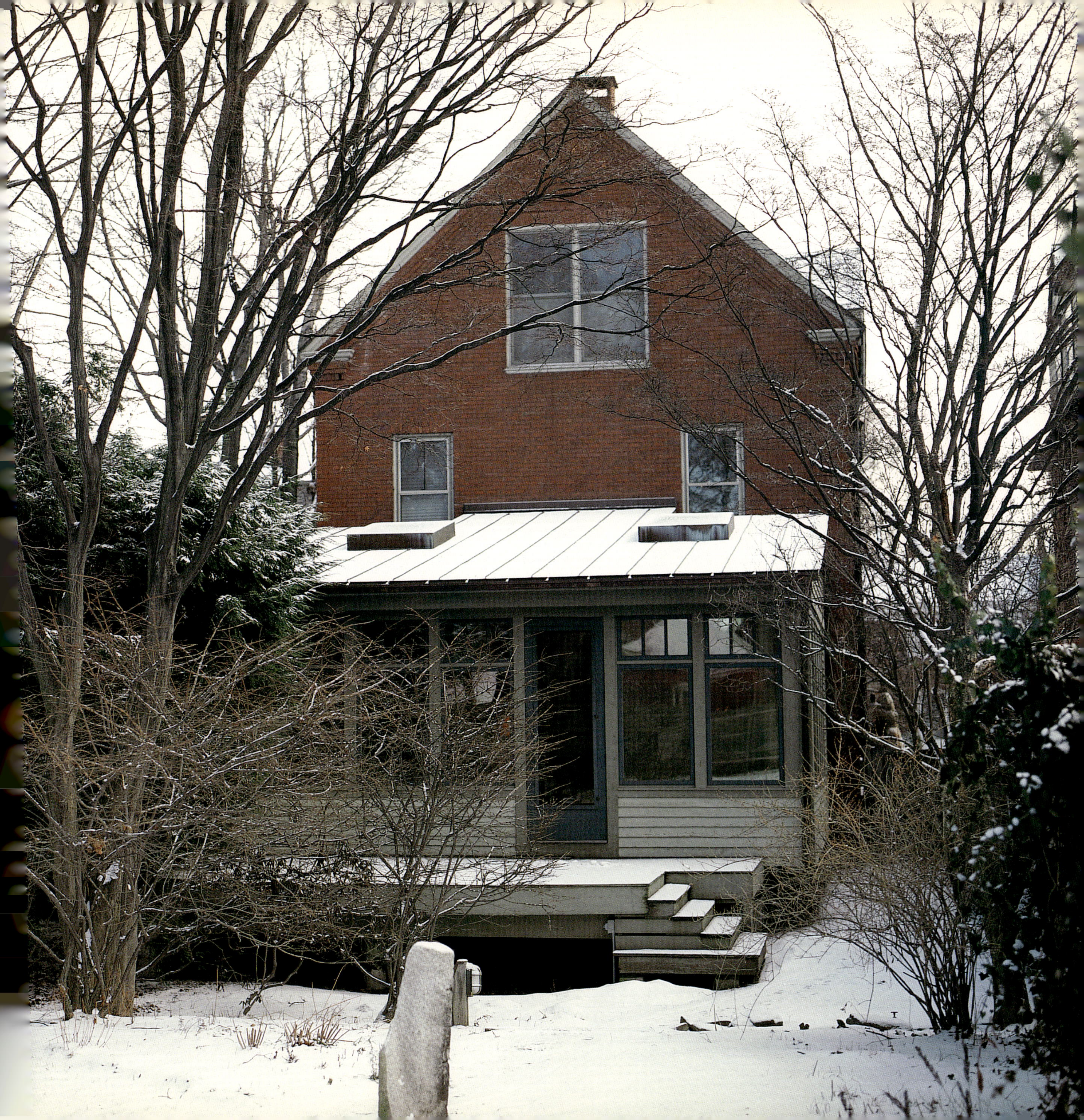

Right: Gathered 'round the living space is a collection of comfortable, clean-lined upholstery pieces and a wooden rocker designed by Hans Wehner.

The round, marble table is a copy that Sam had made, based on one that his parents bought years ago. The marble top is from Barre, Vermont, and reminds Sam of a cloudscape or an ermine robe.

A wall of built-in cabinets houses the television, the children's games, and a thousand back issues of National Geographic.

Sam's command of watercolors would probably allow him a fine living as an artist. He began painting watercolors out in the open fields with his father when he was five. His two watercolors propped against the cabinets are paintings of Thetford Hill in Vermont. The painting on the right is the post office next to their house there, and the one on the left is the church in Thetford. The model of a church atop the cabinets is also the church on Thetford Hill. Sam and Jane were married there, as were Jane's parents back in the thirties.

CITY DWELLING 163

Above: The kitchen is as efficient and trim as a fine boat's galley and offers a view straight through the dining area on out to the neighborhood beyond. "Long views, especially in a city, put the mind to rest," says Sam.

This new kitchen was a partial rehash of the original kitchen. When Sam and Jane purchased the house, the cabinets were natural birch finished with a dark varnish. All the appliances were harvest gold.

Green was chosen for the countertops because the family loves the reminder of the woods. The yellow tones above the cabinets are a memory of many trips to Italy, but the Van Dams' oldest son calls it "macaroni and cheese."

BRING MAINE HOME

- Get rid of your blinds and add sheer curtains—if any at all—to your windows to let more light in your home.

- For your next renovation, seek the ideas of a professional architect; the fees will be worth the creative solutions you'll come up with together.

- Create warm, informal table settings with brightly woven placemats.

- Place a "thinking bench" by your back door.

- Create decorative fronts to your shelves and drawers and let them be part of your living-space décor.

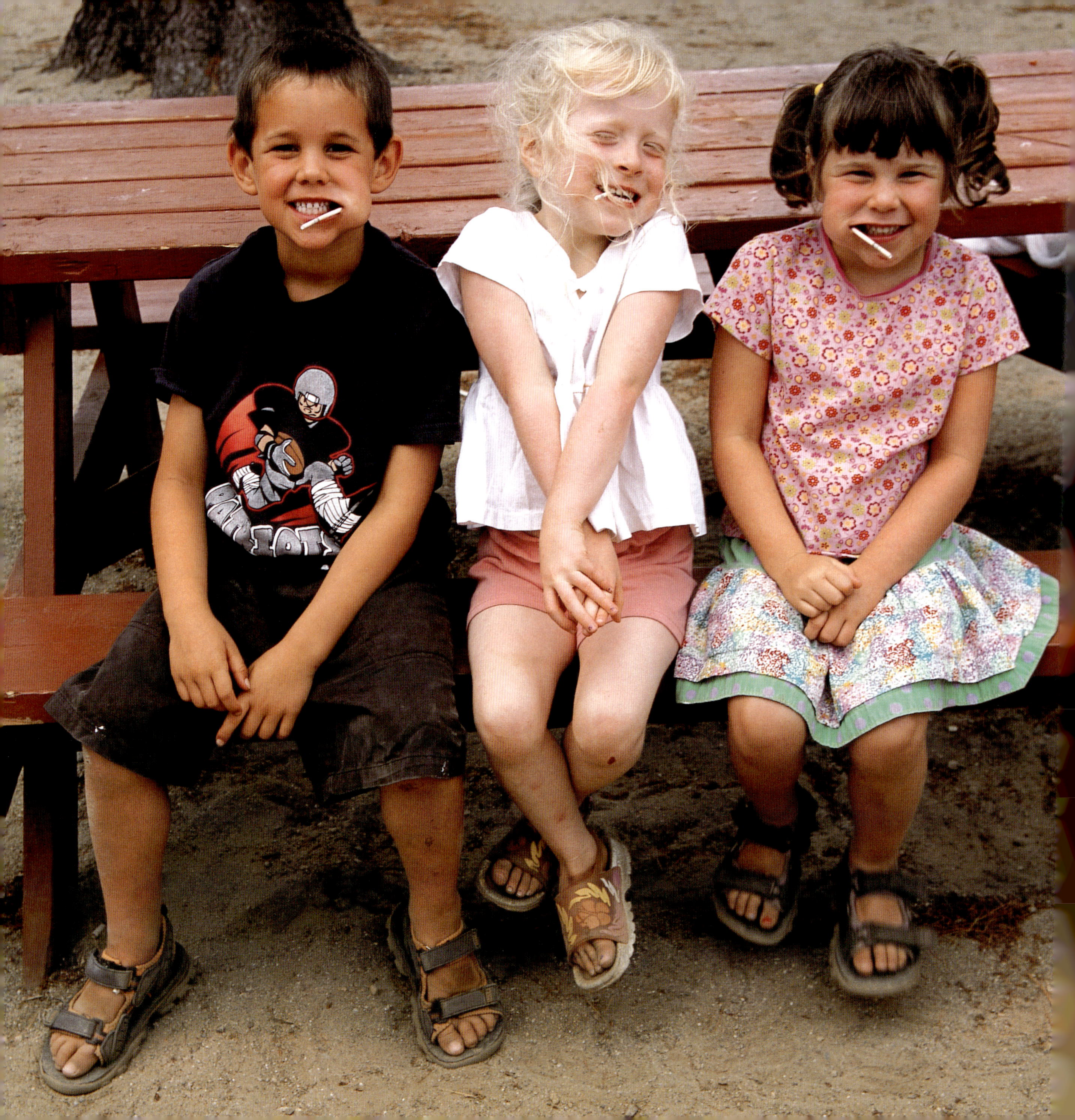

SUMMER FESTIVALS

Parties That Celebrate Community

Maine comes alive after the long winter with a fair and festival activity that rivals a disturbed ant mountain. From the first sign of summer right through autumn, the state is like a giant pasture of fireflies, each glow lighting the way to another celebration. From Grand Lake Stream to South Paris to Millinocket to St. Agatha, summers in Maine become a volunteering bonanza, where smalltown people work together presenting events that honor the bounties and beauties of life in Maine.

Left Page: Silas, Susie, and Mazie enjoy a bluegrass festival in Hiram.

Right Page: Vinalhaven Harbor and docks on a foggy Fourth of July.

Above: The Vinalhaven Rescue Team poses after the island's Fourth of July celebration.

Right: The Common Ground Country Fair is a blanket invitation to experience solace and find peace in an autumn field. Sixty thousand fun-loving visitors head up to Unity each fall to reconnect with rural living, to join in this feast for the senses, and to participate in a down-home celebration of the season's harvests: organic apples and squash, sunflowers and late-blooming perennials, fresh berry pies, homemade honeys and jams, and the best cottage cheese and goat's cheese this side of heaven.

SUMMER FESTIVALS 169

170　Maine Living

Left, Above: The Maine Organic Farmers and Gardeners Association sponsors the fair each year on the third weekend after Labor Day. Spread out over thirty-five acres of old potato fields, now tended with perennials, walkways, and orchards, the best of Maine's folk artists and craftspeople exhibit their products alongside organic farmers and their products. Exhibition tents are filled with such delights as pottery, sweaters from locally spun wool, beeswax candles, jewelry, and elegant soaps.

BRING MAINE HOME

- Attend your local county fair and support local farmers.
- Order a ring or necklace from a local craftsperson.
- Start a yearly tradition of apple-picking.
- Plant your own organic garlic and leeks.
- Let yourself be inspired by the bright colors of a community festival. Note what catches your eye and find ways to use those colors in your home.

SUMMER FESTIVALS 171

172   Maine Living

Left: The Frida Bus, run by a group called The People's Free Space, tours schools, fairs, and festivals to present sustainable alternatives to fossil fuels. Frida Bus is their mobile biodiesel-powered community space.

Above: Organically grown squashes and gourds are an inspiration of shape and color.

SUMMER FESTIVALS

Resources

Dining

The Burning Tree Restaurant
71 Otter Creek Drive
Otter Creek, ME 04660
207.288.9331

Cook's Lobster House
68 Garrison Cove Road
Bailey Island
Harpswell, ME 04079
207.833.2818

Day's Crabmeat &
Lobster, Inc.
1269 Route 1
Yarmouth, ME 04096
207.846.3436

Harbor Fish
9 Custom House Wharf
Portland, ME 04101
1.800.370.1790
www.harborfish.com

Harraseeket Lunch and
Lobster Company
South Freeport Pier
South Freeport, ME 04078
207.865.3535

Jordan Pond House
Park Loop Road
Acadia National Park
Bar Harbor, ME 04609
207.276.3316

Jordan's Snack Bar
Hancock Road
Ellsworth, ME 04605
207.667.2174

Kristina's
160 Center Street
Bath, ME 04530
207.442.8577

The Porthole Restaurant
20 Custom House Wharf
Portland, ME 04101
207.780.6533

Shelter

Blueberry Hill Farm
Bed & Breakfast
101 Old Madden Road
Jefferson, ME 04348
207.549.7448
www.mainefarmvacation.com

Castle Island Camps
Belgrade Lakes, ME 04981
207.495.3312
www.castleislandcamps.com

Chesuncook Lake House
Chesuncook Village
Greenville, ME 04441
207.745.5330
www.chesuncooklakehouse.com

The Claremont Hotel
Southwest Harbor, ME
04679
1.800.244.5036
www.acadia.net/claremont/

The Grey Havens Inn
PO Box Seguinland Road
Georgetown Island, ME
04548
1.800.431.2316
www.greyhavens.com

The Maine Idyll Motor Court
325 Route 1 North
Freeport, ME 04032
207.865.4201

Monhegan House
Monhegan Island, ME 04852
207.594.7983
www.monheganhouse.com

Quisisana
Kezar Lake
Center Lovell, Maine 04016
207.925.3500
www.quisisanaresort.com

Festivals

Bluegrass Festivals
www.maineinfo.net

Common Ground
Country Fair
Maine Organic Farmers and
Gardeners Association
PO Box 170
Unity, ME 04988
207.568.4142
www.mofga.org

Yarmouth Clam Festival
Yarmouth Chamber of
Commerce
162 Main Street
Yarmouth, ME 04096
207.846.3984
www.clamfestival.com

Products

Atlantic Blanket Company
Swan's Island, ME 04685
1.888.526.9526

Barter Family Gallery
Box 102
Sullivan, ME 04664
207.422.3190
www.barterfamilygallery.com

Belle of Maine
W. S. Wells and Son
PO Box 109
Wilton, ME 04294
207.645.3393

The Big Chicken Barn
Route 1
Ellsworth, ME 04605
207.667.7308
www.bigchickenbarn.com

Brahms Mount Textiles
19 Central Street
Hallowell, ME 04347
207.623.5277
www.brahmsmount.com

Center for Maine
Contemporary Art
162 Russell Avenue
Rockport, ME 04856
207.236.2875
www.artsmaine.org

Cornish Trading Company
19 Main Street
Cornish, ME 04020
207.625.8387
www.cornishtrading.com

Damariscotta Pottery
PO Box 211
Damariscotta, ME 04543
207.563.8843

The Farnsworth Art Museum
16 Museum Street
Rockland, ME 04841
207.596.6457
www.farnsworthmuseum.org

Luce's Maple Syrup
54 Sugar Maple Drive
Anson, ME 04911
207.696.3732
www.mainemaple-producers.com

Lunaform
66 Cedar Lane
Sullivan, ME 04664
207.422.0923
www.lunaform.com

Maine Antiques
Dealers Association
www.maineantiques.org

The Maine Blanket
Hatchtown Farm
82 Sproul Hill Road
Bristol, ME 04539
207.563.5952

Maine Cottage
Lower Falls Landing
Yarmouth, ME 04096
207.846.1430
www.mainecottage.com

Orphan Annie's
96 Court Street
Auburn, ME 04210
207.782.0636

Rock Paper Scissors
78 Main Road
Wiscasset, ME 04578
207.882.9930

Sam Shaw
Contemporary Jewelry
Main Street
Northeast Harbor, ME
04662
207.276.0716
www.mainecrafts.org

Stonewall Kitchen
Stonewall Lane
York, ME 03909
1.800.207.JAMS
www.stonewallkitchen.com

Tom's of Maine
P.O. Box 710
Kennebunk, ME 04043
1.800.367.8667
www.tomofmaine.com

Nature

Island Institute
386 Main Street
Rockland, ME 04841
207.594.9209
www.islandinstitute.org

Maine Island
Trail Association
328 Main Street
Rockland, ME 04841
207.596.6456
www.mita.org

The McLaughlin Foundation,
Garden and Horticultural
Center
97 Main Street
South Paris, ME 04281
207.743.8820
www.mclaughlingarden.org

Farms

Apple Acres Farm
365 Durgintown Road
South Hiram, ME 04041
207.625.4777
www.appleacresfarm.com

Nezinscot Farm
RR 2 Box 1311
Turner, ME 04282
207.225.3231

Professionals

Carol Bass Design
314 Littlejohn Island
Yarmouth, ME 04096
207.846.5414
www.carolbasscottage.com

John Silverio
PO Box 725 Proctor Road
Lincolnville Center, ME
04849
207.763.3885

Maine Writers and Publishers
Alliance
1326 Washington Street
Bath, ME 04530
207.386.1400
www.mainewriters.org

Van Dam Architecture
and Design
66 West Street
Portland, ME 04102
207.775.0443